Creative
PAINT FINISHES
FOR THE HOME

PHILLIP C. MYER

NORTH
LIGHT
BOOKS

Cincinnati, Ohio

A NOTE ABOUT SAFETY

Due to toxicity concerns, most art material manufacturers have begun labeling their products with proper health warnings or nontoxic seals. It is always important to read a manufacturer's label thoroughly when using a product for the first time. Follow any warnings about not using the product when pregnant or contemplating pregnancy; about keeping it out of the reach of children; or about mixing incompatible products. Always work in a well-ventilated room when using products with fumes.

The information in this book is presented in good faith but no warranty is given, nor results guaranteed, nor is freedom from any patent to be inferred. Since we have no control over physical conditions surrounding the application of products, techniques and information herein contained, the publisher and author disclaim any liability for results.

CREATIVE PAINT FINISHES FOR THE HOME

Copyright © 1992 by Phillip C. Myer. Text and illustrated artwork by Phillip C. Myer except as otherwise noted. Photographs copyright © 1992 by Russell Brannon Photography except as otherwise noted. Printed and bound in Hong Kong. All rights reserved. No part of this book may be reproduced in any form or by any electronic or mechanical means including information storage and retrieval systems without permission in writing from the publisher, except by a reviewer, who may quote brief passages in a review. Published by North Light Books, an imprint of F&W Publications, Inc., 1507 Dana Avenue, Cincinnati, Ohio 45207; 1-800-289-0963. First edition.

This hardcover edition of *Creative Paint Finishes for the Home* features a "self-jacket" that eliminates the need for a separate dust jacket. It provides sturdy protection for your book while it saves paper, trees and energy.

Library of Congress Cataloging-in-Publication Data

Myer, Phillip C.
    Creative paint finishes for the home / by Phillip C. Myer. — 1st ed.
      p.   cm.
    Includes index.
    ISBN 0-89134-433-0
    1. House painting. I. Title
TT323.M94   1992
698'.14—dc20   92-14214
                                           CIP

Edited by Julie Wesling Whaley
Designed by Carol Buchanan

The listing of credits and acknowledgments on page 136 constitutes an extension of this copyright page.

This book is dedicated to the decorative artists who have come before me and have inspired and influenced my work:
Peter Hunt
Peter Ompir
Joyce Howard
Robert Berger and
Joan Johnson.
And to my teachers who have guided me down the creative road:
Priscilla Hauser
Noreen Banes and
Edith Gould.
To my fellow artist friends who continue to inspire me through collaborations:
Chris Williams
Carol and Tony Myer
Ann and Andy Jones
Joyce Beebe and
Gretchen Cagle.
And to the memory of a dear friend, Fred Walker, who will be greatly missed.

About the Author

Phillip C. Myer has been a decorative artist for more than eighteen years and holds a Bachelor of Fine Arts degree from the University of the Arts in Philadelphia, Pennsylvania. He is the author of eight books on tole and decorative painting and serves on the editorial board of *Decorative Artist's Workbook* magazine. A member of the Society of Decorative Painters for fifteen years, Myer has taught decorative painting seminars across the United States. He currently owns and operates PCM Studios, an Atlanta-based firm specializing in custom-painted interiors and furniture.

INTRODUCTION

Welcome to the world of creative paint finishes: "tricks" that will allow you to paint fanciful textures or duplicate the look of exotic wood, fabric or marble in your home. In this book, painted finishes and decorative painting techniques have been broken down into step-by-step demonstrations that take you through learning to use the tools, mastering the techniques, and developing ideas for decorating floors, walls, furniture and accessories.

You may think, "Oh, but *I* can't do that. That takes talent." Well, let me put your mind to rest. All the techniques taught in this book can be rendered successfully by the novice. Some are quite simple. With a little patience and practice, you can master any of the looks displayed in this book. Take time to thoroughly read and understand each chapter and progress along with the book. If you are a beginner, don't start with the advanced techniques or you might get discouraged before you even get going. Always remember, no one develops his or her skills overnight. Time and practice—with a good deal of trial and error—will fine-tune your painting skills. Don't let the errors slow you down; they will simply become the foundation blocks you'll build on as you work toward a successful painted finish or decorative design.

The techniques within will allow you to become a do-it-yourself decorator.

You can transform old furniture or dated interior spaces with fresh coats of paint, a painted finish and/or decorative design to create a totally new environment. You probably have a few furniture pieces in the attic or basement that need some type of refurbishing. Well, get them out of storage and revive them with the techniques of painted finishes and decorative painting to create heirlooms of tomorrow.

Creating your own painted finishes and decorative design work can save you a lot of money and add value to whatever you are working on. Instead of purchasing wallpaper for your home, create a painted finish and add a decorative stencil. Forget purchasing a piece of painted furniture or a decorative accessory; create one yourself instead.

Once you get hooked on the joys of painting, every surface in sight will become your canvas to create a colorful painted effect. You'll be amazed at your achievements once you learn these techniques and will soon share your newfound love of the decorative arts with others. May I wish you luck on your travels down the path of painted finishes and decorative painting.

Phillip C. Myer

CHAPTER 1. HISTORY OF PAINTED FINISHES AND DECORATIVE ART

PAINTED FINISHES

The art form of painted finishes has evolved into today's looks and standards from a long history of creative effects. The "old masters" of eighteenth and nineteenth century Europe performed painted effects that many call faux finishes today. In times when surfaces such as exotic woods or marbles were not easily accessible, patrons would commission artisans to reproduce those looks on interior surfaces.

Later, in the Victorian era of the late nineteenth century, it was considered prestigious for the upper class to hire an artisan to create painted finishes in their home. In most cases, although materials such as real mahogany or green serpentine marble may have been available, it was actually more in vogue to have the painted reproductions.

Along with traditional painted finishes of woodgraining and marbleizing, stenciled designs were popular for walls, ceilings and floors during the Victorian era. The stenciled designs were not like today's decorative patterns but rather were elaborate and ornate graphic patterns. The colors were vivid, creating an exciting environment.

The early twentieth century saw a growing demand for Victorian-style painted effects in America. The 1920s brought on further development of painted finishes during the Art Deco period. Painted faux finishes were applied to interior surfaces, but a strong design element played a key role in this era. Strong, hand-painted graphic patterns along with stenciled ones trimmed multicolored walls. Artisans painted stripes, bands and borders of color on furniture, walls, floors and ceilings. Along with this graphic use of color, they painted on these surfaces illustrative designs such as female figures. The Art Deco period brought together the talent of painted finish artisans with that of illustrators and fine artists.

Painted finishes waned in popularity in interior decoration in the 1940s through the 1970s. The Depression, the streamlined look of the '50s, the "mod" period of the '60s and the chrome-and-glass era of the '70s eliminated the use of fancy, decorative work in most environments. It wasn't until the 1980s when a strong momentum began to build and painted finishes for interior decoration became extremely popular in America once again.

Today, we are able to mix an array of painted techniques, from those that are centuries old to effects developed only recently. The current eclectic era allows us to mix and match many decorating styles and periods of furniture for a rather unique look.

DECORATIVE ART

The history of decorative art that relates to decorative painting, or what was then called tole painting, dates back to the sixteenth century. *Tole*, the French term for tinware or metalware, was originally used to define the surface itself. But as years passed, the term came to mean a style of decorative painting. Tole painting, the decoration of tinware, was begun in France by a group of nuns who decorated household utensils and containers to brighten up what were dull and unattractive surfaces.

The decoration of functional surfaces developed not only in France but in other European countries at the same time. As the young country of America developed, it too created forms of decorative painting. Heavily influenced by the European immigrants, the decorative painting in America developed a "melting pot" style. Decorative painting styles remained pure only for a short period as one generation passed information to the next. In the New World, original European styles of painting blended together, and American artisans were greatly influenced by their new environment (the landscapes, newfound freedoms, etc.).

The area from New England to Pennsylvania saw the greatest development of decorative painting. The German and Dutch immigrants in this region were the most prolific decorative artists in the New World. These decorative painters, known today as the Pennsylvania Dutch, greatly enhanced decorative painting. The decoration of functional forms was perfected to an exacting art form. These artisans not only

The roots of decorative painting can be seen through early tole painted pieces, such as the document box, upper right. The oil lamp with painted strawberries was painted by Peter Ompir and the stroke- and heart-painted bread tin below was by Peter Hunt, both important twentieth century decorative artists.

painted interior surfaces but also decorated exterior surfaces, such as painted window shutters and the ever-popular Pennsylvania Dutch hex sign used to decorate barns.

A more sophisticated decorative art form developed in New England, where there were active harbor ports. The imported silk, porcelain, and hand-painted furniture and accessories from Europe could be found here. For those who could not afford the European imports, a close duplicate was rendered by the local artisans, who were constantly perfecting their skills.

Two of the most important decorative artists of the twentieth century were greatly influenced by this New England heritage: Peter Hunt and Peter Ompir. A prolific decorative artist, Hunt painted from the 1920s to the 1950s using a bright, bold style.

Hunt eventually settled in the Provincetown/Cape Cod area of Massachusetts, where he saw painted antiques

from the European decorative roots and began developing his own style of the European peasant-style painting. A full-time business developed in which he and staff members transformed old furniture and accessories into revived jewels. His artwork is highly collectible and sought after by many decorative arts patrons today.

Ompir painted around the same time as Peter Hunt (1930s to 1970s) but created a totally different style. Like the itinerant artisans of previous centuries, Ompir left Pennsylvania in the '30s to move to New York City, where he began to decorate functional objects such as cigarette boxes and English tea cans, selling them through an agent. He later settled in western Massachusetts, where he continued to paint and sell his decorative work of fruits, flowers, birds, whimsical figures and animals. His original pieces are very collectible, and continue to inspire decorative artists.

Today, a whole new generation of

decorative artists has developed from the influences of past centuries. A testament to decorative painting's popularity can be seen in the growth of the Society of Decorative Painters. This membership organization is devoted to the promotion of decorative painting through seminars, conventions, expositions and instructional publications. The SDP was formed in 1972 with twenty-two members at its first meeting and today boasts a worldwide membership of more than 30,000. SDP welcomes painters, teachers, retailers, designers, wholesalers and publishers involved in the art form of decorative painting.

The history of painted finishes and decorative painting provides you with the influences and foundation to create another level in the development of these decorative art forms. The combination of painted finishes and decorative painting go hand-in-hand to create an exciting environment in your home.

CHAPTER 2. BEFORE YOU BEGIN

BASIC SUPPLIES

Using high-quality tools is critical in creating effective painted finishes and decorative design work. Of all the tools listed in this section, your brushes are the most important. Just as you can't cut food with a dull, worn knife, you can't paint with poor brushes. If you must skimp to save money, do it with just about any supply other than brushes. Many of the brushes used in this book are expensive, but if cared for and used properly, they can give you a lifetime of painting pleasures.

BRUSHES

You'll need several types of brushes for the techniques taught in this book.

They are divided into three categories: house painting brushes (found at hardware stores), artists'/design brushes (found at art and craft stores) and faux finish brushes (found at art supply stores).

HOUSE PAINTING BRUSHES. These basic, inexpensive brushes (in the $1 to $15 range) are used to base coat surfaces, apply varnishes, paint random color application and block in color. A *base coat bristle brush* is a natural, white bristle brush that is 2 inches wide. *Sponge brushes* are made from foam with plastic or wood handles. They come in 1-, 2- and 3-inch sizes. *Interior wall brushes* are made from a blend of natural and polyester bristles; they come in

3- and 5-inch sizes. *Trim brushes* are made from a blend of natural and polyester bristles and come in 1- and 2-inch sizes. *Varnish brushes* are made from natural, soft bristles and come in 1- and 3-inch sizes.

FAUX FINISH BRUSHES. These specialty brushes are designed solely for particular painted finish effects such as marbleizing, strié, moiré, glazing and more. They are manufactured in Europe and are of high quality. These faux finish brushes are extremely expensive (in the $40 to $250 range) but you really must invest in them if you are serious about this type of painting. House painting brushes are fine for experimenting, and you may get a general feel

for the potential results of a technique. But when it comes time to complete a painted finish on a valued surface, only faux finish brushes will do. *Bristle softener brushes* are made of pure white bristles; they come in 3- and 4-inch sizes. A *badger softener brush* is made from pure badger hair and comes in 2-, 3- and 4-inch sizes. A *bristle flogger brush* is made of pure animal hair bristle and comes in 3-, 4-, 5-, 6- and 9-inch sizes. A *spalter brush* is made of white bristles; it comes in 4½-, 6- and 7-inch sizes. ARTISTS'/DESIGN BRUSHES. The artists' brushes that create the decorative design, stenciling and trompe l'oeil work must be of professional grade. These brushes must be able to perform to your specifications to achieve effective results. If you plan to complete your decorative work in acrylics, then synthetic fiber brushes are best. If you plan to paint in oil or alkyd colors, then fine kolinsky red sable brushes are required. For the paint finishes in this book, you will need these shapes and sizes: *rounds*, nos. 1 and 3; *liner or scroll* no. 1; *flats* nos. 2, 4, 8, 10, 12 and 20. You'll also need two other kinds of brushes: *mop brushes* made of soft bristles that come in ¾- and 1-inch sizes; and *stencil brushes* made from white, stiff bristles that come in ½- and 1-inch sizes.

PALETTE KNIFE
You'll need a palette knife with a long, flexible blade for mixing colors on the palette surface. It also comes in handy when using putty and spackling compounds.

PALETTE
Use a palette pad measuring 12 by 16 inches with a small hole (for holding) to place artists' colors. You'll need a wax-coated palette for acrylics and a parchment paper palette for oils and alkyds.

SPONGES
You need natural sea sponges as well as synthetic kitchen sponges to create some of the painted finishes in this book. A natural sea sponge is one of the most inexpensive yet versatile tools you can use to achieve some incredible results. Each side of the natural sponge will create a different paint effect. Sea sponges are available in art and craft, and hardware stores. Not as versatile as the natural sponge, synthetic sponges can be useful with some painted finish techniques.

CHICKEN OR DUCK FEATHERS
Crisp, white chicken or duck feathers are used in most marbleizing techniques. They must have a fine, pointed tip to create the vein structures in the marble finishes. You can use a feather many times before it wears out and you need to discard it. Buy packages of feathers at art and craft stores or through mail-order outlets (see Sources, pages 134-135).

WOODGRAIN TOOL
The woodgraining tools come in many formats, from the handle to the roller styles. Each produces a different type of woodgrain. The most popular graining tool creates a pattern that duplicates heart of pine. You'll stroke this tool over a wet glaze to make its mark. Woodgraining tools are sold at art and craft stores or via mail-order outlets.

COMBING TOOL
Combs come in many sizes, each with a unique set of teeth marks. Combs may be metal as well as rubber, and can be used to comb, woodgrain or moiré a surface by stroking over a wet glaze. Buy combs at art and craft stores or through mail-order outlets.

TOOTHBRUSH
Yes, you'll need an old toothbrush during the painting adventures in this book for techniques such as flyspecking and granite. Load the brush with thin paint to develop these effects.

PENCILS AND ERASERS
A handful of pencils whose leads vary from 2B to 4H will come in handy when designing, sketching and transferring decorative designs. A large, white artists' eraser will also be very helpful.

TAPES
Several types of tape will aid in the painting process. *Painter's mask-out*

tape is a brown paper tape with a mild adhesive on one half of one side. You'll use it to mask areas you don't wish to paint. *White artist's tape* is a high-quality, mildly adhering tape used to mask out small sections of surfaces when painting around them. *Clear, repositionable tape* is a tape that can be placed on a surface, picked up easily and moved elsewhere. Use it for stenciling and pattern transferring.

RULING PEN

A ruling pen is a tool mainly used by draftsmen and graphic technical illustrators. A ruling pen can be filled with drawing inks, acrylic, oil and latex paints to create fine line work. It is used for the masking/ruling techniques on furniture and accessories.

RAISED RULER

When working with the ruling pen, you'll need a 12- or 24-inch raised ruler. Raised rulers have cork backing along the center of the back of the ruler, leaving the edges of the ruler raised off the surface. This will prevent any paint seepage when stroking the ruling pen along its edge.

CRAFT KNIFE

This style knife is a versatile tool that is good to have. It can be used when scoring a painted and masked/taped edge, for cutting stencils out of Mylar, and for scratching fine lines into painted designs.

STENCIL CUTTER

A stencil cutter is an electric tool with a metal tip that heats up to easily cut through Mylar sheets. It is a valuable tool when designing and cutting out elaborate, large stencil designs.

PERMANENT MARKER

You'll need a fine-line, black, permanent marker when creating your own stencils or tracing decorative designs. In stenciling, you'll use it to draw pattern match-up lines on the Mylar stencil. For pattern tracing, it creates a clean, fine line to follow when transferring your design to the surface.

SANDPAPER

Gather an assortment of sandpaper grades for preparing and finishing your painted surfaces. You'll need all-purpose sandpaper in coarse, medium and fine grades. Wet sanding is required when finishing a surface with varnish. For this you'll need black, silicon carbide wet/dry sandpaper in grits of #400 to #600.

HARDWARE TOOLS

For distressing a painted surface, have on hand the following: hammer, screwdrivers, nails, screws and chains.

MACHINE SANDERS. Heavy-duty machine sanders such as a belt sander, surface sander and floor sander will be needed when tackling large furniture surfaces and flooring. Along with these sanders, you'll need corresponding sanding belts or pads of various grits, from coarse to fine.

PUTTY KNIFE. You'll need a putty knife for applying wood putty or plaster patch compounds to damaged, recessed sections of furniture and interior surfaces. Use a four-inch width for small surfaces or eight-inch width for larger areas.

PAINT STIRS. Have a dozen wooden paint stirs on hand to mix latex and enamel paints that come in quart or gallon containers. The stirs are also handy when mixing large quantities of color glazes for applying to interior surfaces.

PAINT SPRAYER. A professional paint sprayer can be purchased at a hardware store for base coat painting large pieces of furniture and interior surfaces such as walls and ceilings. These paint sprayers come with nozzles that are designed for specific paint types; be sure to use the nozzle for the type you are using.

VACUUM

A vacuum will come in handy when completing painted finishes on floors. You'll do some sanding when preparing the floor surface, which will create a good deal of dust to vacuum.

PAINTS, VARNISHES AND MEDIUMS

One of the most exciting parts of painting is being able to work with the richness of color, sheen and texture. Five paint types are used in this book: oils, enamels, alkyds, acrylics and latex. Each has its own characteristics and benefits for using it to complete the painted finishes and decorative design work.

The choice of paint type in some instances is a personal decision; at other times, though, a specific type will create the easiest and most effective result. Here's a list of paint types and colors used in this book, and a list of the techniques that work well with each.

ARTISTS' OIL COLORS. A professional grade of oil color is made of ground powder pigment in linseed and other oils. It is packaged in tubes in a thick consistency. Artists' oil colors' solvent is turpentine. Artists' oil colors are recommended for the following techniques: antiquing, woodgraining, all marbleizing, all decorative painting, tortoiseshell, malachite, trompe l'oeil and fantasy finishes. Oil colors can also be used as color glazes with these techniques: ragging, texturizing, glazing, strié and moiré. Here are the colors needed to create the techniques in this book:

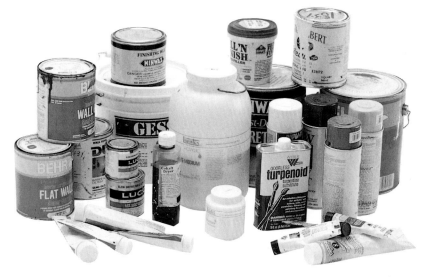

asphaltum	leaf green light
burnt alizarin	mauve
burnt sienna	Payne's gray
burnt umber	permanent green
cadmium orange	light
cadmium red light	Prussian blue
cadmium red	raw umber
medium	titanium white
cadmium yellow	ultramarine blue
medium	viridian
ice blue	yellow ochre
lamp black	
leaf green dark	

ARTISTS' ACRYLIC COLORS. A professional grade of acrylic paint is made from powder pigment ground in acrylic polymer emulsions. It is packaged in tubes in a thick, creamy consistency. Artists' acrylic colors' solvent is water.

Acrylic colors can be used successfully in the following techniques: sponging, flyspecking/granite, masking/ruling, stenciling, trompe l'oeil and decorative painting. These acrylic colors were used in this book for flyspecking and granite and for blocking in trompe

l'oeil:

burnt sienna	raw umber
burnt umber	titanium white
lamp black	warm gray
Payne's gray	

ARTISTS' ALKYD COLORS. The alkyd painting medium combines the benefits of both oils and acrylics. The alkyds will handle in similar fashion to oils, allowing you to blend and work with them for awhile due to their open time. Yet they will dry to touch in about eight hours. A professional grade of alkyd color is made from powder pigment ground in synthetic resin derived from glycerol and phthalic anhydride. It is packaged in tubes in a thick consistency. Artists' alkyd colors' solvent is turpentine. You can use alkyds in the following techniques: all marbleizing, decorative painting, trompe l'oeil and fantasy finishes. If you use alkyds for these techniques, gather the colors listed under "Artists' Oil Colors."

ENAMELS. Oil-based enamels are a liquid mixture of powder pigments plus resins, hydrocarbons, driers and additives. They are packaged in pint, quart and gallon cans. Oil-based enamels' sol-

vent is mineral spirits. Semigloss oil-based enamels are highly recommended for many of the techniques in this book—they are ideal for interior surfaces such as floors, walls and ceilings. Enamels are used for base coating and in paint glazes for these techniques: ragging, texturizing, glazing, strié and moiré. They can be used in just the base coating stage for the following techniques: all marbleizing, antiquing, woodgraining, gilding, decorative design, tortoiseshell, malachite, trompe l'oeil and fantasy finish. The color choice will be personal for the first group of techniques; the following colors are needed for the second group of techniques:

black	tan/beige
light emerald	white
green	

LATEX. Latex is a paint made from powder pigment ground with an emulsion of rubber or plastic globules. It is packaged in pint, quart and gallon cans. Latex paints' solvent is water. Latex wall paints are ideal for several of the paint finish techniques, including: sponging, flyspecking, crackling, distressing, masking, ruling and stenciling. The color choice will be a personal one. A flat paint is recommended for furniture and walls; a semigloss is ideal for woodwork and doors.

You can mix several of the paint types to create the painted finishes. Oils, enamels and alkyds can be used together on the same surface. Acrylic and latex paints can also be mixed.

SPRAY PAINTS. Spray paints are good for priming and base coating smaller surfaces such as accessories. Metal surfaces require rust-preventive paint; the spray can produces the best result on this surface. You can stencil with spray paints as well, but use extreme control during the aiming and painting.

GESSO. An acrylic, polymer-based emulsion, gesso is an excellent primer product. Traditionally used for priming artists' canvases, gesso is highly recommended for priming furniture and accessory surfaces. It seals and primes the surface, preparing it for any type of painting technique to be applied over it. It creates a semiporous surface, so you may need additional sealing, depending on the technique.

WOOD SEALER. When working a raw wood surface, a wood sealer may come in handy. The resin-based clear wood sealer will close the wood pores so your paint coating over it will not soak into the surface. It also will seal over knotholes, preventing them from yellowing through your painted finish later.

VARNISHES. To preserve your painted finish or decorative design, coat the surface with several applications of a varnish. The varnish product comes in the following types: oil-based varnish, lacquer-based varnish, polyurethane-based varnish and water-based varnish. Each has its own set of benefits and disadvantages. The type of painting technique and surface usage will dictate which varnish to use. See chapter nine for more information on varnishes.

CLEAR PAINTING GLAZE. You'll see clear painting glaze listed in the materials needed to create many of the painted effects taught in this book. The clear painting glaze is a "homemade" product you'll make yourself with a mixture of dammar varnish, turpentine and linseed oil (see page 9).

COBALT SICCATIVE DRIER. Cobalt siccative is added very sparingly to oil colors to aid in the drying process. Using too much of it will cause the paint to crack as it dries. If you pour it into an eye dropper, you can easily add just a few drops to your paint mixtures as needed.

PAINTING MEDIUM. A painting medium is used to thin the consistency of your paints (oils, alkyds, acrylics). Each paint type has a corresponding painting medium. A painting medium is usually made up from the binders and solvents used to create and thin the given paints. For example, an oil painting medium can be made up of linseed oil (the binder) and turpentine (the solvent). There are several painting mediums on the market for oil and alkyd colors. Add the desired amount to thin down paint to an applicable consistency.

MISCELLANEOUS MATERIALS

You will need various materials to prepare and complete the painted finishes and decorative design work. Gather the following items:

tracing paper pad, 12 by 16 inches
graphite and white transfer paper
scrap white paper for testing
sheet of glass, 12 by 16 inches
clear Mylar sheets, 12 by 16 inches
tack cloths
plastic drop cloth
cheesecloth
rubber sanding block
plastic-weave scrub pad, 3½ by 5 inches
metal paint tray with plastic liners
mineral spirits
turpentine
lacquer thinner
imitation gold or silver leaf, in books of 5½ by 5½ inches, twenty-five sheets
leaf sizing, quick or slow dry
clear acrylic spray
hide glue
stencils, precut designs
wood putty compound
plaster patch compound
3M's Safest Stripper
naval jelly
paste wax
brush creme

HOUSEHOLD ITEMS

Collect the following household items to use in some of the painted techniques:

cardboard box (shoe box)
large plastic or glass jars with lids
coffee cans with lids
aluminum pie pans
plastic containers to hold solvents (to clean brushes)
white, mild bar of soap
plastic wrap
newspapers
cotton balls and cotton swabs

absorbent, soft paper towels
100 percent cotton rags/cloths (old
    T-shirts are ideal)
scraps of cardboard

Basic How-To's

There are a few basic principles you'll need to understand before beginning to paint any of the techniques in chapters four, five, six, seven and eight. Read the following information to prepare yourself for the painting adventures that lay ahead.

Making a Painting Glaze

A clear painting glaze is required in many of the painted finish techniques. It's economical to make this glaze yourself, since you'll need large quantities of it. Make a large jar of the painting glaze to have on hand before you begin painting.

To make this glaze, purchase the following items at an art or craft store: dammar varnish, pure linseed oil, and turpentine. Get at least 32 ounces of each item. In a large container, such as a clean bucket, mix with a paint stir equal amounts of the varnish, linseed oil and turpentine. Now, pour it into a couple of plastic or glass jars and close tightly with lids. This clear painting glaze will keep for a couple of months. After that, if the glaze has been sitting unused, it is better to mix a fresh batch.

Cleaning Your Brushes

The care of your brushes is crucial to their life. If you don't thoroughly clean the brushes after you are done painting, you can ruin them. Follow these simple steps to cleaning brushes, and they will last a long time.

HOUSE PAINTING BRUSHES. This brush type should be thoroughly cleaned in the paint's solvent until no sign of color comes out of the brush. Then use a mild soap and water to remove any excess color or solvent. Shake off excess moisture and allow to dry.

FAUX FINISH BRUSHES. This brush type should be thoroughly cleaned in the paint's solvent until no sign of color comes out of the brush. Use soap and water only on the flogger, bristle softener and spalter brushes. Don't use soap and water on the badger softener brush. Water will bloat the badger hairs.

RED SABLE ARTISTS' BRUSHES. This brush type, used for oil and alkyd painting, should be thoroughly cleaned in turpentine until no visible color comes from the brush. Then coat the brush with brush creme and form it into a natural shape. Remove creme with turpentine before painting again.

SYNTHETIC ARTISTS' BRUSHES. This brush type, used for acrylic painting, should be cleaned thoroughly in water to remove all color from the brush's hairs. Clean with soap and water as well. When completely clean, stroke the damp brush across a bar of soap and shape soap into the brush's natural form. Rinse the bristles in clean water to remove dried soap when beginning to paint again.

Developing Paint Consistencies

To create the painted finishes and decorative design work, you'll need to thin the paints into various paint consistencies. You'll use either the paint's solvent, clear painting glaze or painting medium to thin down the paint. There are four basic paint consistencies used throughout this book: thick, creamy consistency; thin, creamy consistency; thin, soupy consistency; and ink-like consistency. Here is how to create these consistencies:

THICK, CREAMY CONSISTENCY. Add a few drops of thinning agent and whip with a palette knife. The paint should be thick enough to form peaks when you pat the palette knife over it.

THIN, CREAMY CONSISTENCY. Add a medium amount of thinning agent to the paint. Mix with a palette knife to the consistency of whipped cream.

THIN, SOUPY CONSISTENCY. Add a large quantity of thinning agent to the paint. Mix with a paint stir to a creamy, tomato soup-like consistency.

INK-LIKE CONSISTENCY. Add a lot of thinning agent to a small amount of paint. As the name implies, you'll mix paint to the watery consistency of ink.

CHAPTER 3. SURFACE PREPARATION

You cannot expect to achieve quality results with your painted finish or decorative design work if you have not taken the time to properly prepare the surface below your work. A smooth, sealed surface is required to create any of the painted finishes and decorative painting techniques taught in this book. In most cases, a poorly prepared surface will only be magnified once you apply the painted technique on top. So, although the preparation of the surface may seem the boring part of the painting project, it will pay off in the long run.

PREPARATION OF INTERIOR SURFACES

You need to complete a few preparatory steps on interior surfaces (walls, ceilings, floors, doors and woodwork) to get them ready to accept the painted finish. The condition, the age and the painted technique to be applied to the surface will determine the approach you'll take during the preparation stages. Walls, ceilings, doors and woodwork are prepared in similar manner, while floors have their own requirements.

WALL AND CEILING PREPARATION

Begin by reviewing the wall or ceiling surface. Look for imperfections such as nail holes, indentations or nicks that need to be filled with plaster patch. Also, check to be sure drywall or plastered walls are in good shape. Determine the cause of any flaking or peeling. If leaking water is the culprit, the leak must be fixed first. Plastering or painting over a leak will not solve the problem.

PATCHING AND SANDING. Once you have located the irregularities in the surface, you must fix them. Circle small imperfections with a pencil during your inspection. This will help you remember where they are later when you go to plaster them. Using spackling compound and a putty knife or palette knife for small areas, stroke on a sufficient amount of plaster over the recessed imperfections. Apply a little extra, due to shrinkage during drying. For extremely large areas that need plaster, build them up gradually with several layers of plaster, allowing each coat to dry between

---

KEYS TO SUCCESS

❧ Be sure to fill in all surface imperfections such as nail holes with putty or plaster patch. The painted finish techniques will not hide imperfections; they will simply magnify them.

❧ Start sanding with a coarse to medium grade of sandpaper and work down to finer grades. The coarser grades will take off rough areas quickly, while the finer sandpapers will finish smoothing the surface.

❧ A sealed, nonporous surface is essential before completing any of the painted finishes or decorative design work. A surface can be sealed with paints, varnishes or sealing products.

❧ Strip a surface only when there is no other solution. Stripping is such a big mess that the piece of furniture must be somewhat valuable to you to be worth the effort.

❧ The approach you take to priming the surface should relate to how you plan to finish it. Before spraying, brushing or rolling on the base coat paint, determine your painted finish technique. This will likely dictate the type of base coat application required. (See Base Coat Application on page 12, and read the preparation steps for each technique you want to complete.)

Materials needed:
Oil enamel, acrylic latex and concrete paints
Wood sealer
Oil-based wood primer
Gesso
White oil enamel primer
Large house painting brushes, detail trim brushes, base coat bristle brush
Rollers and paint trays
Masking tape and plastic
Coarse-, medium- and fine-grade sandpapers
Sanding block
Machine sanders
Wood putty and spackling compounds
Putty and palette knives
Drywall primer
Tack cloths
Paint stirs
Paint sprayer
Mineral spirits or water as solvent
Vacuum
Plaster

SPACKLING WALLS AND CEILINGS

Minor valleys or nail holes in the wall or ceiling will need to be filled in with several applications of plaster patch or spackling compound. Apply a generous amount of compound with a putty knife, allowing for shrinkage during drying.

SANDING WALLS AND CEILINGS

You'll need to sand walls and ceilings to even out the plaster patch and any minor bumps or "tooth" texture in the surface. Use a sanding block and a medium grade of sandpaper first, and finish by sanding with a fine-grade sandpaper.

applications. Allow plaster to dry according to the label's instructions. Sand the plastered area until you achieve a smooth surface. If some shrinkage occurred in the drying process, apply additional plaster, let dry and sand again.

If the drywall or plaster on the wall is flaking or peeling, scrape loose areas off with a putty knife. Be sure to remove all the loose stuff or else new paint will not adhere well. Sand flaky areas with a coarse sandpaper on a sanding block. Try to level out the areas between the flaked-off paint and the flat surface areas. Apply a coat of plaster patch over recessed areas, let dry, and sand with medium and fine grades of sandpaper until smooth.

PRIMING. If you are working on newly constructed walls, you'll need to prime the drywall with two coats of drywall primer. Due to its thin consistency, this primer can be rolled or brushed on regardless of the painting technique you are going to complete. Sand the surface lightly with a medium or fine grade of sandpaper after the coating of primer is thoroughly dry.

If you are changing the wall color from a very dark color to a light one, a primer coat of white is suggested. Apply the white paint over the existing dark tone. One to two coats is sufficient — you don't need to achieve an opaque coverage. Simply lay down a priming coat that will make it easier to cover with the top base coat color.

Always stick with the same type of product throughout the priming and base coating part of the project. If you elect to use a water-based product such as latex or an oil-based product such as enamel, use that same type of paint for priming and base coating.

Oil-based enamels are best as the primer and base coating paint for most of the techniques in this book except for sponging, granite or flyspecking, and stenciling, where water-based products work best. The benefit to the oil-based enamels is that they seal, prime and prepare the surface, allowing you to complete any type of painted finish or decorative design work on top without the paint penetrating the base coated surface.

BASE COAT APPLICATION. The base

coat application is an important step in the painting process. It will create a foundation for the painted finish you apply on top of it.

Before you begin, thoroughly mix the paint with a paint stir. Mix well, but don't cause such friction that a lot of air bubbles form.

Whether you base coat with a brush, roller or spray can, apply two or more coats until you achieve an opaque coverage on the wall or ceiling surface. Allow each coat of paint to dry thoroughly before applying another. Sand lightly between coats if the surface raises a rough grain or tooth. Use a fine grade of sandpaper and remove sanding dust with a tack cloth.

Brush-on Base Coat. The following techniques require a base coat application with the use of a brush: glazing, antiquing, crackling or distressing, masking or ruling, decorative design, woodgraining, strié, moiré, all marbleizing, gilding, tortoiseshell, malachite, trompe l'oeil and fantasy finishes.

When base coating with a brush, use as large a brush as you feel comfortable with for the area being base coated. Always stroke in long, sweeping strokes from top to bottom. Overlap previous paint strokes onto joining areas, and always be on the lookout for paint runs.

Roll-on or Spray-on Base Coat. The following techniques require a base coat application with the use of a roller or spray: sponging, ragging, texturizing or plastic wrapping, granite or flyspecking, and stenciling.

To paint a wall or ceiling with a roller, you'll first need to use a small, detail trim brush to paint all areas that you won't be able to reach with the roller. Brush around all baseboards, moldings, windows, doors and corners. Now you can quickly roll on the remaining areas. Pour paint into a paint tray, load a fine-textured roller with paint, and roll on the surface. Be careful not to build up a thick coating of paint that will run down the wall. Roll on at least two coats of the base coat color to achieve an opaque coverage.

Spraying on a base coat requires a fair amount of preparation, so while you may save in the painting time, you will use a great deal of time in masking first. Spraying paint on walls and ceilings is ideal when working in newly constructed spaces where floors (carpet or hardwood) have not been laid and woodwork and trims have yet to be painted. This allows you to go in with a paint sprayer and sweep around the room very quickly. If the interior is not new construction, however, you'll need to mask windows, trim, molding and floors with plastic and tape. If you dislike brush-on and roll-on base coat painting, the masking stage may seem worth the extra effort; you'll be able to breeze through the spray paint stage. Several paint sprayers are available at your hardware

store. The critical aspect to using these tools is to achieve the proper paint consistency and use the correct spray nozzle. You'll need to thin the paint down from its original state. Use mineral spirits for oil-based paints and water for water-based paints. The paint must be thin for it to flow through the small opening in the nozzle. There is a corresponding paint nozzle for every paint type as you will see when you buy or rent a sprayer. Once you have the paint sprayer loaded with thin paint and the correct nozzle on, begin painting. Start at the top of the surface and work downward, painting a three-foot-wide section at a time. Use a light, sweeping motion, overlapping the previous sweep. Don't attempt to achieve an opaque coverage the first time around; build up gradually to prevent paint runs from forming on the surface.

DOOR AND WOODWORK PREPARATION

There is usually less preparation needed for door and woodwork surfaces than wall and ceiling. Unless you are working on an older home that has a big build-up of coats of paint, you can prepare and prime the doors and woodwork easily. The condition of the doors and woodwork can fit into one of three categories: "new," i.e., raw wood; "middle aged," i.e., stained or painted; and "older," i.e., multilayered painted surface. Each has its own set of preparation instructions. Follow these simple steps and you should have no problems during the painted finish stages.

NEW DOORS AND WOODWORK. When working with raw wood doors and woodwork in newly constructed homes, you'll need to seal and prime the surface before base coating. A wood sealer product will close the pores of the wood, creating a nonporous surface for the paint to be brushed over. A wood sealer will also prevent any knotholes from yellowing and showing their age through the paint surface later. Apply one to two coats to the raw wood surfaces with a sponge or bristle brush. A quality wood sealer will raise the grain once it has dried on the surface. Simply remove this slight roughness with a sanding block and a fine grade of sandpaper. Remove sanding dust with tack cloth. For best results, prime the surface with gesso if you'll be using water-based paints, or with a white oil enamel primer for oil-based paints. The primer paints seal the surface properly and provide an opaque coverage as a starting point for your base coat. After one coat of primer paint, sand lightly and remove dust with a tack cloth. After the primer coat is brushed on the surface and sanded, you can build up an opaque coverage of the desired base coat color.

MIDDLE-AGED DOORS AND WOODWORK. To prepare a middle-aged door or woodwork surface (a surface that has been stained or painted only a couple of times), sand the surface with a medium grade of sandpaper to provide a tooth to the surface for better paint adhesion. Remove sanding dust with a tack cloth and apply a coat of primer paint. Sand lightly after the primer paint is thoroughly cured (dried) and wipe with a tack cloth. Now, apply the desired base coat on the door/woodwork surface.

OLD DOORS AND WOODWORK. When working on older doors and woodwork in poor condition, level out the surface as best you can. Usually in older homes, surfaces have a build-up of different levels of paint and, along with this, some wear and tear may have occurred, causing chipping and flaking on the surface. You'll need to first sand the surface with a coarse grade of sandpaper to level out the layers as much as possible. If large areas of paint are missing, causing deep recesses, build them up again with paint, plaster patch or wood putty. Apply one of these to areas that need building up, let it dry, sand the surface with a medium-grade sandpaper, and remove dust with a tack cloth. Now, sand over the entire surface with medium-grade sandpaper to provide a tooth to the surface. Remove sanding dust with a tack cloth. Coat with a primer paint and base coat with the desired color.

Stripping doors or woodwork should only be attempted when they are in dire shape. Stripping is a very large undertaking and is extremely messy. If you do attempt stripping, you must go all the way down to the bare surface. Once the surface is totally stripped, you can treat its preparation like it is a raw wood surface. For more information on stripping wooden surfaces, see pages 16-17.

BASE COATING DOORS AND WOODWORK. When base coating doors and woodwork, you'll need to brush on the paint; using a roller or paint sprayer are not viable options. Use trim brushes for painting woodwork and a larger brush for base coating the doors. Sand after the first base coat, wipe with a tack cloth, and then apply several more coats until opaque.

FLOOR PREPARATION
When creating painted finishes or painted designs on floors, it is critical that you achieve good paint adhesion and add a quality protective finish over your work. The most ideal floor surface to work on is raw, new wood flooring. This allows you a fresh surface to start the project. If you don't have new floors to work on, that doesn't mean they can't receive a painted finish. You'll just need to prepare them with slightly different methods.

To prepare raw wood flooring, seal the surface before applying any paint. Brush on a coat of wood sealer, allow it to dry, and sand it. Remove sanding dust with a vacuum and tack cloths.

Leveling Out Doors and Woodwork

Sanding Floors

When working on old doors or woodwork, level out previous layers of paint as best as you can by filling in recessed areas with spackling compound or new layers of paint. Then sand the surface to even up these areas and create a tooth to the surface for new paint adhesion.

Floor surfaces such as heart of pine need some type of sanding, from fine sanding for new floors to heavy-duty sanding for older floors. Use some type of machine sander such as a belt sander for touch-up sanding or use a professional floor sander for overall sanding. After machine sanding, finish with some fine hand sanding in areas that need it.

Now, prime the entire floor surface with a white oil enamel primer. Let it dry, and sand again. Remove dust with a tack cloth. Base coat the floor with several coats of base color. Now you're ready to grid off a tile design or draw whatever pattern you've chosen and create a painted finish.

Floors that have been previously stained, varnished or painted will need to be lightly sanded to create the tooth for new paint adhesion. A professional floor sanding machine is recommended. Be careful when using these machines because they can take a level of flooring down in very little time. Use the finest grade of sandpaper pad to create the tooth to the surface. Only if the floor surface is in very bad condition should you use heavier grades of sanding pads. Sand out any gouges or imperfections in the flooring with these heavier grit sand pads. Then finish sanding with the fine pad. Vacuum the dust, and wipe with a tack cloth. Next, prime the floor surface with a white oil enamel primer. Let it dry and lightly sand the surface. Remove sanding dust with a tack cloth. Paint the base coat next, applying several coats of color. Grid off the floor with your pattern, and create the painted finish.

Masonite and sub-flooring surfaces can receive a painted finish, too. Simply seal these surfaces, sand, prime and base coat as instructed with the wood floor surfaces. Remember, if the surface has already been finished, sand to create a tooth to the surface for good paint adhesion.

Another flooring surface, concrete, can also be painted. Basements, porches, sunrooms and some covered exterior entryways are made with concrete flooring. These surfaces are ideal for painted finish techniques to dress them up. Treat raw concrete flooring with special concrete paints that seal the surface and also seal moisture out. If moisture is trapped in concrete and gets between the layers of paint, you'll get poor paint adhesion. Base the floor with these concrete paints, then you can use oil enamels or artists' oil colors on top to create the painted finish.

If the concrete is already painted and good paint adhesion is evident, apply a fresh coat of concrete paint and complete the desired painted finish. If there are any chipping and flaking areas of the concrete paint, scrape off all loose areas and recoat those places with fresh paint. Try to build up these areas with paint to level out the surface to be painted. Sand the whole surface lightly and remove dust. Recoat the entire floor with fresh concrete paint, let dry and create the painted finish.

To complete any type of painted finish on wood floors, you'll need to prime the wood flooring with several coats of an oil-based primer. Brush on a smooth application, let dry and sand lightly. Remove sanding dust with a tack cloth and apply a second coat of primer.

Although an extremely messy task, stripping may be necessary when a furniture surface has many layers of paint or varnish. Apply stripper with an old paintbrush, allow it to activate, and then begin scraping off the surface with a putty knife. Furniture with multiple layers will require several applications of stripper.

PREPARATION OF FURNITURE AND ACCESSORY SURFACES

The beauty of painted finishes and decorative design work is the magic of being able to transform objects such as old pieces of furniture and accessories into fresh, useful items for your home. In your attic, basement or garage there must be at least one piece of furniture or accessory item that has been set aside because it no longer fits into the scheme of your decor. Well, with a few coats of paint and decorative designs or a painted finish technique, it can be brought out of the darkness and shine brightly in your home once again.

You can choose to paint on new as well as old pieces of furniture and accessories. All types of accessories can receive painted finishes, including lamp bases, columns, metalware, candlesticks and more. You can sectionalize a piece of furniture with different paint finishes

KEYS TO SUCCESS

❧ You will need to strip furniture or accessory surfaces when the paint is peeling and flaking badly.

❧ Correct damaged sections of furniture, peeling paint and loose veneer before applying a base coat to the surface. Applying new paint over these problems will not correct them.

❧ Furniture provides one of the most versatile surfaces for the application of an array of base coat choices. Analyze the sections of the surface and plan in advance how you'll finish it.

❧ Accessories are prepared in similar manner to the larger surfaces of interiors and furniture: sand, seal, prime and base coat. You'll need to be a little more detail-oriented due to the intricacies of accessories.

Materials needed:
Oil enamel paint, base coat acrylic paint, latex house paint, spray paint
Gesso

Detail brushes, base coat bristle brush, old paint brush
Wood sealer
Machine sander and sanding belts
Coarse-, medium- and fine-grade sandpapers
Sanding block
Wood glue
Wood putty and spackling compounds
Thin, sharp knife
Putty and palette knives
Plastic wrap or waxed paper
Tack cloths
Stripper, such as 3M's Safest Stripper
Scouring pad (made of coarse plastic weave)
Coffee can
Vinegar and water
Newspapers
Plastic drop cloth
Rubber gloves (for coarse hand sanding, stripping , and cleaning metal in a vinegar bath)
Clear acrylic spray
Naval jelly
Rust-remover product
Rust-preventive metal primer
Wood stain or varnish
White artists' tape

Any gouges or valleys in the furniture will need to be filled in. Apply wood putty with a putty knife or palette knife and mold it to match the surrounding area. Let the compound dry and sand it with medium and fine grades of sandpaper.

by following the furniture's shapes. Trim, molding, recessed panels, leg tips, door panels, filigree work—all can be painted in contrasting colors and paint finishes. Plan this prior to painting your piece of furniture by practicing with colors and techniques on sample boards.

You will probably only refinish a furniture or accessory surface once, so it's definitely worthwhile to take your time and do a quality job, thus creating a family heirloom. Just as with interior surfaces, furniture and accessory surfaces must receive a good foundation for a high-quality painted finish to result. The following sections cover the variety of preparation steps you'll need to complete on furniture and accessory surfaces. The condition of the surface will dictate how it needs to be prepared.

FURNITURE PREPARATION

If the piece of furniture you wish to revive has a heavy coating of varnish, wax, furniture polish or slick paints, you must "cut down" this heavy coating by sanding or stripping the piece of furniture. On smaller pieces, you can probably get away with sanding the surface with an electric sander, but on larger pieces that are badly chipped or flaking, you'll need to strip the paint and varnish layers off the surface.

STRIPPING FURNITURE. There are stripping agents available at hardware stores, such as 3M's Safest Stripper, that are nontoxic and odor free. An alternative to stripping a piece of furniture yourself is to take it to a commercial stripping company.

Stripping furniture is no fun job no matter what product or technique you use, but it can be worth it. First, evaluate the piece of furniture: Do you think this extra amount of work or expense (if you have it commercially stripped) is going to add personal or financial value to the furniture? If you have any doubts that it's worth it, you may want to pass this piece by.

Begin by test stripping a small section, such as a drawer from the piece of furniture. You can see how many layers of paint, varnish or stains are on the piece, how difficult the removal will be, and what type of wood is underneath. Keep in mind that this test area will not be a guarantee of what the entire piece is like. You may have a piece of furniture that was made from scraps of wood and was meant to be painted.

If you've decided to strip the piece of furniture yourself, gather your supplies together. If you use a stripping product other than 3M's Safest Stripper you must work in a very well-ventilated area (outside is ideal), and work away from anything important (flecks of stripper can fall on surrounding surfaces and create an instant disaster). Lay down a plastic drop cloth, then arrange several layers of newspaper. This provides you a total area to discard once you have completed stripping. Position the piece so the surface you work on is horizontal. Brush on the stipper and allow it to activate, lifting up the paint or varnish. Depending on the product and paint or varnish to be stripped, you'll have to wait up to three hours before scraping off the first layer.

Using a putty knife, scrape off the paint and discard it into a coffee can. Next, scrub the surface with a scouring pad coated lightly with fresh stripper. Unless the piece was covered with only one coat of paint, you'll probably have to repeat the process, especially in certain areas where the paint was not loosened with the first treatment. Complete one round of stripping on the entire piece before using a second coat of strip-

PREPARING NEW FURNITURE

Unfinished furniture is popular because you can easily apply any finish you desire. Sand the raw wood with sandpaper, remove dust with a tack cloth, seal it with a coat of clear wood sealer (as shown) or gesso. Let the sealer dry and sand again, remove dust, and prime with a coat of gesso.

per. Continue these steps until all paint and varnish are removed.

Once you have completed stripping and/or heavy-duty sanding with a coarse grade of sandpaper, you must smooth out the surface. Using an electric sander and a fine grade of sandpaper on the belt, sand the entire piece. You'll need to hand-sand curved or detailed areas such as carved sections. After all electric sanding is completed, hand-sand with medium and fine grades of sandpaper. At this point, evaluate the condition of the wood and patch any damaged areas with putty. Let dry and sand. Remove sanding dust with a tack cloth.

REPAIRING DAMAGED FURNITURE. If the piece you wish to work on has a chipped or damaged surface, the veneer is coming loose, or the paint is peeling, follow these steps:

For damaged areas, build up the surface so it's level with the other areas of the piece. Wood spackling compound works well. Using a palette knife, pick up plenty of spackling compound and stroke over the recessed area. Be sure to stroke on excess compound. Now, using the side edge of the palette knife, stroke over the surface to level out the compound. Follow the contour of the area surrounding the damaged area—make it flat or curved. Allow the compound to dry. If any areas of the compound shrink in the drying process, apply additional spackling compound. Sand the area to a smooth surface to match surrounding areas.

For areas of peeling paint, you must either sand the surface or strip and sand the surface. If only some areas of the painted surface are peeling while others are adhering firmly, you can complete heavy-duty sanding and then begin the painting process. If the piece has many layers of paint peeling and flaking off,

you must strip the furniture before beginning to paint.

For furniture with loose veneer, glue down to the surface the veneer that is coming up. Clean out the loose area by slipping a thin, sharp knife into the slot and scraping the old glue. Squeeze wood glue into the slot and press down. Wipe off the excess glue. Cover the area with plastic wrap or waxed paper and apply pressure with a clamp, heavy book or brick. Allow the glue to dry at least four hours, remove weight, and sand glued area lightly.

PREPARING UNFINISHED FURNITURE. To prepare new, unfinished furniture, thoroughly sand the surface with medium and fine grades of sandpaper. Remove sanding dust with a tack cloth. Now, seal and prime the surface to be painted. Gesso is an excellent product to both seal and prime the raw wood surface. Apply several coats and sand to remove roughness from the raised grain. You can also use a commercially made, clear wood sealer to seal the wood.

BASE COAT APPLICATION. Once you have completed these preparation stages, the piece of furniture is ready for base coat application. There are many ways in which you can base coat and prime the piece. Here are a few suggestions:

Full Color. A flat base coat color can be applied to the entire surface using a base coat acrylic paint or flat latex wall paint. Prime the furniture surface with gesso, sand with medium and fine grades of sandpaper, then apply several even coats of base coat paint to the entire surface until you have an opaque surface.

Stained and Painted Areas. You can

easily mix stained areas of furniture with base coated areas. If the piece has many sections that are segmented with molding, recessed panels or decorative trim, you can highlight these areas even more by base coating some places with paint and other areas with stained or natural wood. (See the armoire that's stained and hand-painted, page 125.) Complete the staining first. Then, after the stained areas are dry, mask them off with tape, and paint the solid color areas.

Totally Natural. If the wood grain and the condition of the piece are exceptional, you may consider letting the natural wood show through. Simply varnish the wood to seal and protect the grain, then complete your decorative painting on top. (See the Art Deco-style armoire, page 117.)

Color Trims. A piece of furniture can look great with several different base coat colors applied in trim and border patterns. Choose contrasting colors or use shades of the same color. The best approach is to base coat the entire piece with the lightest tone, then trim with other colors. You can paint these trim sections by using white artists' tape for masking off areas. (See the country-style jelly cabinet, page 121.)

Textured Backgrounds. You can add a great deal of texture to a piece of furniture by creating a sponged, stippled or patterned background. (See the sponged and painted side table, page 120.) This allows you to use hints of many colors in the furniture to tie a room's color scheme into the piece of furniture. This technique also hides a lot of blemishes if the furniture has

acquired them over the years.

Once you have completed the base coat stage on the furniture, lightly seal the stained or painted surface with several mists of clear acrylic spray before beginning the decorative or painted finish steps.

ACCESSORY PREPARATION

You can apply painted finishes and decorative design work to just about any type of accessory piece. If you completed painted finishes on your interior and furniture surfaces, why not complete painted finishes on your accessories for a total coordinated look? The three most typical accessory surfaces are wood, metal or plaster. Follow these simple steps to prepare an accessory made from one of these three surfaces:

PREPARING WOODEN ACCESSORIES. An accessory made from wood will require sanding with medium- and fine-grade sandpapers. Sand the raw or painted surface, then remove sanding dust with a tack cloth. Prime the wood surface with a coat of gesso and let dry. Sand again to remove the raised grain, and base coat with your desired color.

PREPARING METAL ACCESSORIES. An accessory made from metal can be prepared several ways, depending on its condition. For new, unprimed metal, you'll find that it has an oily film on it. Although this prevents the piece from rusting, you can't paint or prime over it. To remove this film, simply soak and wash the piece in a solution of 60 percent water and 40 percent vinegar. Before going any further, make sure the metal is completely dry. Moisture left on the metal will cause rust. Next,

prime your metal. First, place a light coat of naval jelly over the entire surface with a clean cloth or brush. Naval jelly serves as a primer for your metal because it cleans and prepares the surface for paint. After the jelly is dry, apply a rust-preventive primer. You can brush or spray on the primer, but you'll find that spraying metal objects will be easier than tackling them with a brush. Regardless of the method you choose, watch out for paint runs and brush marks. Also, be sure to let the primer dry at least twenty-four hours.

If you wish to paint an accessory piece that is rusty, don't despair. Once you remove all the rust from it, you'll be amazed at how paintable it becomes. If your piece is extremely dirty and oily, wash it in the vinegar and water solution. Then apply any commercial rust-remover product (sold in most automotive supply stores), and your rusty piece will become as good as new. When using any rust-remover, be sure to read the package carefully, as instructions vary from product to product. Also, keep in mind that heavy-duty rust may take several applications. Once the rust is removed, you can apply a rust-preventive primer. On pieces that were heavily rusted, use three applications of primer.

Once the metal is primed, the next step is to base coat with your background color. Again, you may either spray or brush on your paint, although a spray paint is ideal for the metal surface. If you use a spray product, be sure to thoroughly shake the can first. When spraying, hold the can 12 inches from your metal piece. Move in a sweeping motion from side to side, then up and down to achieve smooth, even coverage. Avoid spraying layers of paint too quickly—it's better to apply several light coats (allowing each to dry) than one heavy coat that will run.

PREPARING PLASTER ACCESSORIES. An accessory piece made from plaster requires similar preparation steps to those that are needed for wood priming and sealing. First, however, you need to make sure your surface is clean. You'll find a coating of dust on most plaster forms, so be sure to wipe it off with a tack cloth, taking special care to clean all crevices. Once the plaster is clean, prime it with gesso. Plaster is extremely porous, so this step is very important. You don't want your paint to bleed into the surface. Because the plaster will absorb the first two coats of gesso, you'll need to apply at least three coats before the surface pores are saturated and a seal begins to form.

Apply the layers of gesso with a soft, synthetic bristle brush appropriate to the size of your surface. On very detailed and multidimensional pieces, use a small brush for covering recessed areas of the mold. Be sure to let each coat dry at least one hour, then sand the surface lightly and wipe it with a tack cloth before applying another. Once the plaster is primed with gesso, lightly mist the surface with several coats of clear acrylic spray. Allow it to dry, and base coat with your desired color.

PRIMING A METAL ACCESSORY

New or old metal accessory pieces require a cleaning bath of 60 percent water and 40 percent vinegar to remove dirt and oils. Dry the metal off and then coat with a rust-preventive metal primer. A spray-on primer is the easiest to work with when painting metal surfaces.

SEALING PLASTER ACCESSORIES

The porous surface of plaster must be sealed and primed before you do any type of painting. The best primer for plaster is gesso. Sand the surface with fine sandpaper, remove dust with a tack cloth, and apply at least three coats of gesso to prime the plaster surface. Then, lightly mist the surface with clear acrylic spray.

CHAPTER 4. EASY PAINTED FINISH TECHNIQUES

Sponging
Ragging
Plastic Wrap Texturizing
Granite and Flyspecking
Glazing
Antiquing
Crackling and Distressing
Masking and Ruling

The eight techniques in this chapter are best described as simple, beginning-level effects a novice can master easily. These basic painted effects are all abstract, except the granite technique. By abstract, we mean they are not out to mimic a realistic surface (such as marble in the technique of marbleizing). These eight techniques create texture, patterns and color tones on any surface you desire.

Read through all eight techniques and follow the step-by-step photographs. If you are a beginner to painted finishes, choose one of these eight easy finishes to experiment with and to develop the feel of the paint and tools. All eight techniques are rated at a similar basic level; practice them to establish confidence before attempting the intermediate- or advanced-level techniques.

SPONGING

Due to its loose, textural qualities, sponging provides an ideal backdrop for almost any interior style. Sponging is well suited for kitchens, bedrooms and bathrooms. The technique can be used on furniture as well as on walls, but on furniture it looks best combined with another technique. Complementing techniques that work well with sponging on walls or furniture include stenciling, masking or ruling, and basic decorative design.

Sponging can be completed in several different effects. Transparent paint application uses very thin paint: water-based paints thinned with water or oil-based paints thinned with mineral spirits. Transparent sponging is best suited for an overall even pattern effect.

Opaque application uses paint that has not been thinned. By simply adjusting the color values you use, you can create a variety of effects. For a soft look, choose a base tone and top color that are very close in value, such as beige and white. If you desire more contrast in the finished effect, choose three colors in a range of values (such as light blue, medium blue and dark blue; or light yellow, medium blue and dark green).

Opaque sponging can be used to create a random pattern like transparent sponging, or a more controlled, flowing pattern. A flowing pattern is abstract—it should be evident but not so extreme that the shapes jump out at you. Work at a diagonal to the surface and alternate starting at the bottom and starting at the top.

The sponging technique can be completed in three distinct styles: transparent sponging at left, opaque sponging in the middle, and flowing pattern sponging at right.

PREPARATION

To create any sponging technique on a surface, apply an opaque base coat of paint. Apply several smooth coats with a brush or roller. If there are surface imperfections, sponging hides a multitude of sins.

TRANSPARENT SPONGING

STEP 1. Thin the paint to an ink-like consistency. Thin latex and acrylic paints with water; oils, enamels and alkyds with mineral spirits. Moisten the sponge with corresponding thinner, squeeze out the excess, and load the sponge with the thinned paint mixture. Lightly pat the surface with the sponge.

STEP 2. To even variations in the color values, repeat color application after the first application is dry. Multiple colors in transparent sponging can be achieved by lightly sponging over a second color after the first is thoroughly dry.

OPAQUE SPONGING

STEP 1. Apply with either a brush or sponge the lightest color you've selected as the base coat. Allow it to dry. Moisten the sponge with corresponding medium and squeeze out excess moisture with several paper towels. Apply the medium tone to the surface. Complete the overall application of this color, and allow it to dry.

STEP 2. Wash out the sponge, remove moisture, and load it with the dark tone. Sponge over the surface at random, allowing the light value as well as the medium value to show through the dark application. Allow it to dry.

STEP 3. Complete the opaque sponging technique by "knocking back" the medium and dark values. Use a sponge to apply the first color (lightest tone) to the whole surface. This will even out any paint blotches you may have created on the surface.

KEYS TO SUCCESS

❧ When loading the sponge, always dip it in the color as evenly as possible. One area of the sponge loaded with excessive paint can cause ugly splotches.

❧ Always test the sponging pattern on a scrap surface (such as paper) before applying color to your real surface. This will help you detect any heavy areas, as well as remove some excess paint.

❧ Rotate your sponge after making each mark on the surface. This will prevent any distinct line-up of pattern repetition.

❧ Dab the sponge on the surface in a random overall pattern. Don't apply sponge marks in a row.

❧ When working on vertical surfaces such as walls, watch out for paint runs, especially with transparent sponging. Small runs are acceptable, but sponge over any runs longer than a quarter of an inch.

Materials needed:
Acrylic, latex, oil, enamel or alkyd paints
Water or mineral spirits (for thinning)
Natural sea sponge
Paintbrush (for base coating)
Paint trays
Paper (for testing)
Paper towels

FLOWING PATTERN SPONGING

Complete Steps One and Two of opaque sponging. After completing the dark tone application and allowing it to dry, load the sponge with the lightest color. Now, instead of applying that color overall, pick out specific areas for color application. Sponge on color in a diagonal, curving shape that starts out small and progressively gets larger.

RAGGING

The ragging technique is another loose, carefree effect that creates an unusual patterned backdrop for many environments. Ragging is a mottled, textural pattern created with a transparent glaze of paint. Like sponging, ragging has variations to try, such as rag rolling and flowing pattern ragging. Ragging is a comfortable look in the elegant setting of a living room as well as in a country-style kitchen. This technique is effective on walls, ceilings and sections of furniture; complementing techniques that work well with ragging include masking or ruling, woodgraining, and gilding.

The ragging technique is traditionally a three-step process of applying a base coat, applying a glaze, and creating a mottled pattern. This technique creates a two-tone coloration on the wall. You may choose to repeat the last two steps of the three-step process for a multicolor look.

PREPARATION

Base coat the surface to be ragged with several coats of oil enamel. It will look better if you use a paintbrush instead of a roller. Allow it to dry for at least forty-eight hours. Once the base coat is thoroughly cured, you can begin ragging. Mix one part enamel or artists' oil color to three parts painting glaze in a jar. You want to create a transparent color glaze that will allow the base tone to show through. Pour the glaze mixture into a paint tray.

The ragging technique is an exciting textural look whether you choose standard ragging (left), rag rolling (center), or flowing pattern ragging (right).

KEYS TO SUCCESS

❧ A critical element to ragging is the consistency of the glaze. If the glaze is too thick with color, you'll lose the nice two-tone effect of the base coat showing through the glaze. On the other hand, if you mix too much painting glaze with the paint, the surface will dry too quickly, become tacky, and it will be difficult to develop a rag pattern.

❧ Work only on one manageable section of the surface at a time—3 square feet at first. As you become more proficient, you can try working on a slightly larger area.

❧ Your base coat should be a good solid, opaque coverage. The ragging is semitransparent and will allow the base to show in many places.

❧ You can stop after ragging one glaze application, or you can apply a second glaze and rag again for a pattern-on-pattern look. Make the second glaze slightly more transparent than the first by using more painting glaze in the mixture.

❧ Plan in advance the flowing pattern ragging. You'll need to work on a large area at a time, so it's best to work with an assistant.

❧ For flowing pattern ragging, divide the task into a two-step procedure. Your assistant will work closely ahead of you, applying the glaze to the wall, while you go behind creating the ragged pattern. Try to rag one area at a time, using an area 8 feet wide by the surface's tallest dimension.

Materials needed:
Semigloss oil enamel and/or artists' oil color paints
Mineral spirits (for cleaning up)
Cotton rags
Large jar
Clear painting glaze
Base coat bristle brush

RAGGING

STEP 1. Once the glaze has been applied, pick up the rag and compress it into an irregular shape. Begin patting randomly, creating marks in the glaze surface. Be sure to overlap marks and keep ragging until you can't see any brushstrokes.

STEP 2. Continue the rag marks beyond where you stopped the glaze application, softening this edge to prevent distinct lines from showing between sections. Continue this method over the entire surface.

RAG ROLLING

STEP 1. Rag rolling is not very different from ragging. Base coat the surface and apply the glaze. Instead of using a wadded-up rag, roll a rag into a cylinder and roll it over the surface. Use the palms of your hands or even pressure on your fingertips to press and roll the rag across the surface.

STEP 2. Overlap the rows of rolled marks. It's best to roll up and down vertically along a wall surface, and lengthwise across a flat surface such as a tabletop. A second color glaze can be applied over the dried rag rolling, but since this technique is so pattern-intensive, one layer is best.

FLOWING PATTERN RAGGING

STEP 2. Dip a wadded rag in glaze and touch it to a scrap surface to remove any excess. Pat the surface in flowing, diagonal "rivers" spaced out every 6 to 8 feet on a wall. (For smaller surfaces, such as a tabletop, fewer rivers, spaced 12 inches apart, will look pleasing.) Start at the top with a small width, and increase the size as you move downward. If the flowing color area is too distinct, soften it with rags.

STEP 1. Rag over the surface by patting the glaze with a wadded cloth in your hand. Create an overall, even rag pattern quickly so you can go on to Step 2 while the glaze is still wet.

Plastic Wrap Texturizing

The plastic wrap texturizing technique is similar to ragging, but the finished look is harder-edged—a more distinct "alligator skin" pattern results. This effect is best used as an accent or backdrop to other decorative elements. Ideally suited for furniture, the plastic wrap technique can also be used on walls, columns and small accessories. Complementing techniques that work well with plastic wrap texture include marbleizing, elaborate decorative design and glazing.

You can soften the look by executing the ragging technique using a wad of plastic wrap in place of a rag. You'll create an interesting texture pattern but the strong alligator look will not be evident.

Preparation

Base coat the surface with several coats of oil enamel. Allow each coat to dry thoroughly before applying another. Then allow the base coat to dry for forty-eight hours before doing the plastic wrap technique. Mix one part oil enamel or artists' oil color with three parts clear painting glaze in a jar. The paint mixture should be a transparent glaze. Pour the glaze mixture into a paint tray. Tear off a sheet of plastic wrap larger than the area to be glazed, and wad it into a ball. Next, release the pressure and allow the wrap to spread back out.

Plastic wrap texturizing can be completed in two different styles: the alligator plastic wrap method (left) and the ragging plastic wrap method (right).

ALLIGATOR PLASTIC WRAP

STEP 1. Apply glaze to the surface with the base coat brush. Now, allow the glaze to set up and become slightly tacky (about one minute). Pick up the crumpled wrap and place it on the wet, tacky glaze. Pat the surface lightly with the flat of your hand or with even pressure on all your fingers. Pick up the edge of the wrap and remove it.

STEP 2. Move onto the next area. Brush on glaze next to the previously completed area, overlapping the glaze slightly. Allow the glaze to become tacky, and apply a fresh piece of wrinkled plastic wrap. A new pattern will occur each time; don't worry about different patterns or slight variations in color values.

KEYS TO SUCCESS

❧ Work only on a 3-square-foot area at a time.

❧ Control the amount of time you allow the glaze to set up and become slightly tacky. If the glaze is too wet or too dry, the plastic wrap pattern will not hold on the surface. On very wet glazes, the wrap will pull a lot of the color off; on dry glazes, the wrap will pull off very little color.

❧ If you start to get a wide spectrum of color values and patterns from one step area to the next, you are not being consistent in the amount of time you're allowing for the glaze to become tacky. Monitor your time carefully.

❧ To correct inconsistent color values, go over high contrast light and dark areas with a used plastic wrap wad and pat over the surface to blend the colors better.

Materials needed:
Semigloss oil enamel or artists' oil color paints
Base coat bristle brush
Roll of household plastic wrap
Clear painting glaze
Large jar
Paint trays

RAGGING PLASTIC WRAP

Brush on glaze and allow it to set up for about one minute. Tear off a sheet of plastic wrap and wad it up into a ball. Release the pressure on the wrap and begin touching the glaze randomly to create a textured pattern. From time to time, move to a fresh spot on the wrap. Once the piece of wrap is full of paint and no longer makes distinctive pattern marks, discard it and start with a fresh piece. Continue making texture marks beyond where you stopped the glaze application. This creates an irregular shape, which will blend with the new glazed areas.

Granite and Flyspecking

Used alone, these techniques create subtle textural surfaces. You can also combine them effectively by masking off different areas and flyspecking some places with one color, while painting other areas to look like granite. Flyspecking and granite are most effective when used in small doses such as on molding or sections of furniture—they're great for accessory pieces. Complementing techniques that work well with flyspecking and granite include sponging, antiquing, and masking or ruling.

You can use either water-based or oil-based paints for flyspecking and granite, but because these techniques are layered wet over dry, the best mediums are acrylics or latex paints.

Preparation

For flyspecking, simply base coat the surface in any color or stain application you desire. For the granite effect, base coat an opaque coverage with an earth tone such as a warm gray.

You can combine simple flyspecking (left) with the texture of a granite-like finish (right) for an appealing look on furniture and accessories.

Flyspecking

To flyspeck an area, thin the paint to an ink-like consistency. Load the toothbrush with the thinned paint. Now, hold the brush handle in the palm of your hand and wrap your fingers around it as if you were about to make a fist. Place the bristle section near your thumb. Angle the bristles downward, facing the surface, and run your thumb over the bristles, causing flecks of paint to fall onto the surface.

Keys to Success

❧ You have limited control of where and how the paint will fall while rendering these techniques. The best advice is to work with the paint texture that occurs. If you're terribly unhappy with the look, immediately wipe the paint off while it's still wet.

❧ Test the paint consistency on a section of your palette for the size of dots that will fall.

❧ Control the amount of paint flecks by varying how fast you rub your thumb over the bristles. The faster the action, the more the flecks; the slower the action, the fewer the flecks.

❧ You can control the *size* of the paint flecks: the closer you are to the surface, the finer the mist of paint flecks; the farther away you are, the bigger the flecks.

Materials needed:
Latex or acrylic paints in earth tones such as burnt umber, warm gray, lamp black, raw umber and white
Base coat bristle brush
Old toothbrush
Natural sea sponge
Water

Painted finishes are ideal for application on frame as well as mat surfaces. Here, the granite finish was completed in warm earth tones on the frame while the mat has been flyspecked with complementing hues.

Granite

STEP 1. Thin white acrylic paint with water to a wash consistency and brush over the surface with the base coat bristle brush. While the paint is still wet, pat the surface with the natural sponge to create an irregular pattern texture.

STEP 2. Thin with water to an ink-like consistency several shades of earth tones, such as burnt umber, raw umber, warm gray and lamp black. Load your first color onto the sponge and pat it on the surface randomly. Repeat with each remaining color.

STEP 3. Finish by flyspecking the surface with each of the colors used in the painted finish. Start with the white and gray; finish with the browns and black. Flyspeck each color overall, and then pick sporadic areas for strong flyspecking concentration of a particular color.

GLAZING

The term *glazing* is ambiguous. An artist can use paint glazes on surfaces in which to make patterns or marks (ragging and strié); a glaze can be applied over a previously painted design to enhance or modify colors; and a glaze can be applied to give a smooth, lustrous surface. Glazing as a painted finish technique is simply a transparent wash of color over another color. Alone as a painted finish, glazing is ideal for walls, but floors and even ceilings can be glazed. Complementing techniques that work well with glazing include marbleizing, stenciling and gilding.

There are two basic approaches to glazing. The first is an even application of a transparent color over a base tone. The second approach, textured glazing, is the same application of transparent glaze, but imperfections are purposely left in the glaze—imperfections such as paint runs in the glaze itself and texture imperfections in the surface.

PREPARATION

Prepare the surface for glazing by applying several coats of an oil enamel. Allow *each* coat to dry thoroughly. Let the base coat color cure for at least forty-eight hours before applying any glaze.

Create a glaze mixture of oil enamels or artists' oil colors and clear painting glaze. Add one part enamel to four parts painting glaze in a jar. Stir until the mixture is thoroughly blended, then pour into a paint tray.

The subtle look of glazing can be completed in a smooth, slick effect (left) or executed with a rustic, loose finish (right).

The candlesticks with candle followers have a combination of painted effects completed on their surface. The candlesticks have been glazed with a soft yellow tone in the textured technique. The candle follower shades have been gilded in the antique, patina style with burnt umber antiquing.

GLAZING

STEP 1. Load the base coat bristle brush with the paint glaze mixture. Stroke it over the surface, brushing out the transparent glaze until you achieve a smooth coating. The glaze should flow on the surface so the brush marks are not too visible.

STEP 2. Continue to apply glaze to the surface and brush it out. Apply glaze in as large an area as possible at one time. Soften with the badger softener brush while it's still wet. Continue this application over the entire surface.

TEXTURED GLAZING

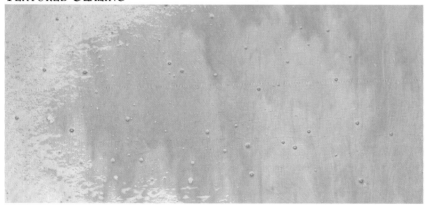

For a more rustic effect to glazing, you can be a little haphazard in the glaze application, allowing brush marks to show and letting paint runs and wall imperfections rear their ugly heads. When brushing on the glaze for this look, you need to exercise very little care or method.

KEYS TO SUCCESS

❧ There is no particular pattern to be achieved from glazing. It is totally an abstract effect, so very little about this technique can be considered incorrect or improper.

❧ Glazing is best achieved with oil-based paints, though on small areas a water-based product could be used.

❧ It is best to brush on the base coat. A rolled-on surface will cause a pebbly look, which shows up in the glazing effect.

Materials needed:
Semigloss oil enamel and/or artists' oil color paints
Base coat bristle brush
Mineral spirits (for cleaning up)
Clear painting glaze
Large jar
Paint trays
Palette knife (for mixing paint glaze)
Badger softener brush

ANTIQUING

You can create a painted finish on a piece of furniture or interior surface today and make it look as if it were completed centuries before. Antiquing, the application of earth tone glazes, can fool the eye into believing a painted surface is much older than it is. Antiquing is ideal for furniture and accessory surfaces but also can be completed on interior surfaces such as walls. Complementing techniques that work well with antiquing include decorative design, gilding and woodgraining.

There are several different levels of antiquing. Subtle antiquing is the softest look and is achieved through minimal application of antiquing mixture on a well-sealed surface. Your goal here is to alter the coloration of the painted finish with a soft, mellow tone. In midlevel antiquing, you leave more antiquing mixture on the surface to "age" the painted surface more. Extreme antiquing is the ultimate in the aging process. It adds years to a painted finish, making

Antiquing can be created in three degrees: subtle (left), midlevel (center) and extreme (right). In these examples, the base coat is a cream tone.

it look as if it were painted a century ago. You can shade, accent and highlight with heavier antiquing, creating a great deal of interest and dimension.

PREPARATION
For subtle antiquing, mix equal parts of burnt umber, burnt sienna and asphaltum. Squeeze paints onto a palette and mix with a palette knife. Create a soupy consistency to the paint by moving the color mixture to a pie pan and adding a generous amount of mineral

spirits. For midlevel antiquing, develop the same earth tone oil mixture described above, but this time add less mineral spirits. You want to create a thick, creamy consistency. For extreme antiquing, make an antiquing mixture that is the consistency of paste. On a palette, mix equal parts of burnt umber, burnt sienna and asphaltum; to this add a few drops of mineral spirits. Whip paint and spirits to a paste-like consistency with a palette knife.

KEYS TO SUCCESS
❧ Protect the painted finish surface before antiquing by coating it with one to two applications of varnish. This way, *you* control the amount of aging, rather than the antiquing process taking over the situation.
❧ When antiquing large areas, break them into sections. Complete all steps on a given section before moving on to the next. The best rule is to work on a maximum area of 3 square feet. Once you are familiar with the technique and have control of what is being

completed, tackle a slightly larger area at a time.
❧ Antiquing is best done in artists' oil colors. The oils allow a great deal of open time, providing you with plenty of time to create the look you desire.
❧ To create antiquing with a range of tones, start with a fresh rag at a spot you would like to become a highlight area. Touch the surface with a heavy amount of pressure and begin moving toward a dark area. As you begin reaching that darker area, release the amount of pressure. In doing this,

you'll begin to create a range of tonal values, from a light area, to a midvalue area, to a very dark area.
❧ If at any time you remove too much antiquing, apply additional color and blend with the rag into existing tones.

Materials needed:
Earth tone artists' oil color paints such as burnt umber, burnt sienna and asphaltum
Mineral spirits
Palette and palette knife
Base coat bristle brush
Varnish and varnish brush
Lint-free cotton rags
Pie pan

SUBTLE ANTIQUING

STEP 1. Using a bristle brush, apply antiquing mixture over a sealed (varnished) surface. Now, using a cotton rag and a circular buffing action, immediately begin to wipe off excess antiquing coloration. You'll wipe off 95 percent of what you have just brushed on to achieve the subtle look.

STEP 2. The antiquing mixture will tend to seep into crevices or imperfections on the surface. For this subtle look, wipe away as much of the antiquing as possible in these areas. This application of antiquing will slightly alter the surface's coloration, enhancing it to a mellow hue.

MIDLEVEL ANTIQUING

STEP 1. Apply the antiquing mixture on the surface with a bristle brush, working it into all crevices. Pick up a cotton rag and lightly wipe over the surface with a circular buffing action. You want to achieve an even color tone over the entire surface.

STEP 2. Allow the base coat to show through the antiquing mixture. The result of this technique should be a midvalue haze of antiquing coloration over the surface. In this type of antiquing, you do not accent or highlight any part of the surface; the whole area has an even, consistent finish.

EXTREME ANTIQUING

STEP 1. Using the bristle brush, stroke the antiquing mixture over the surface. Spread the thick mixture by using a good deal of pressure on the brush. Now, pick up a cotton rag and lightly wipe the surface in a circular buffing action. At this point, you are simply moving around the paste to even out its coverage.

STEP 2. Using a clean area of the rag, begin wiping, with pressure on a potential highlight area. Remove a fair amount of antiquing paste in this area. After you have wiped the paste from these lightened areas, you'll need to create the midtone values between the very dark areas and the light areas (see Keys to Success, page 32).

CRACKLING AND DISTRESSING

Crackling and distressing techniques provide a painted finish with similar "aged" qualities to those of antiquing techniques. The crackled effect provides the illusion that the paint finish has crazed, as many surfaces do when exposed to a variety of elements over a long time. Distressing, simply put, is the battering of a painted surface to provide the illusion that it has received a great deal of wear and tear over the years. Furniture and accessory surfaces are ideally suited for these techniques, but sections of wall surfaces can be crackled and distressed for a rustic, country look. Complementing techniques that work well with crackled and distressed effects include decorative design, antiquing and woodgraining.

The crackled finish allows you to achieve a two-value tone of the same color or create a two-color finish. The crackled finish shows the base color below, providing the two-tone effect. You can use antiquing over a crackled finish, enhancing the illusion of age.

In distressing a surface, you either sand, make dents and marks, or scrape into the finish to give the worn and weathered look. Just about any destructive tool will work when distressing a surface. Screwdrivers and screws are ideal for scraping random marks into the painted finish. Pound the head or tip of a screw with a hammer to make marks. Or, lay the screw on its side and tap on the surface with a hammer to get the side pattern of the screw. Small chain links like the ones you hang plants with are great distressing tools. Simply

The crackled finish (left) adds texture as well as years to a surface, while the distressing finish (right) makes the surface look as if it has gone through years of wear and tear.

hold the chain on one end while you hit the surface with the other end.

PREPARATION

To create a crackled finish, first achieve an opaque coverage by base coating the surface with several coats of acrylic base coat or latex paint. Allow it to dry. Next, pour hide glue into a pan and add a small amount of water. Mix with a palette knife.

To create a distressed look, finish a surface with a painted technique or solid color application. For worn effects giving the illusion that the surface has been handled a great deal, use sandpaper as the distressing tool. For a rougher look, use tools to mark the surface.

KEYS TO SUCCESS

❧ When creating the last stage of the crackled finish, you can only brush over a given area once. More than once will lift off the crackled paint effect.

❧ When brushing on the paint to crackle, use as large a brush as you feel comfortable with and cover as large an area as possible. You stroke the paint over the dried glue. As you do so, the paint will begin to immediately separate, forming the cracks.

❧ When distressing, the only thing that could go wrong is that you get carried away and distress the surface more than you meant to. So hold back when trying this for the first time.

Materials needed:
Acrylic or latex paints
Base coat bristle brush and sponge brush
Hide glue
Pan and palette knife
Water
Medium- to coarse-grade sandpaper
Hammer, screwdriver, nail, screw, chain and other destructive tools

CRACKLING

STEP 1. Brush the hide glue mixture over the entire surface with a sponge brush; allow it to dry.

STEP 2. Choose your top color. As you brush on the top coat, align each stroke of the brush so you don't overlap the strokes. Do *not* overstroke an area, or you'll pull up the paint. You can adjust the type of cracks slightly by the amount of paint on the surface. A thin coating of paint will create a fine, close grouping of cracks; a thick coating, as shown here, will create larger cracks.

DISTRESSING

STEP 1. Your goal is to cut through the top coat to show the coats below. With a piece of medium-grade sandpaper, begin sanding at the edges and in the center of the surface. On painted wood surfaces, sand through the paint down to the raw wood or colors below. For additional wear, use a coarse grade of sandpaper.

STEP 2. For an added destructive look, pick up a large, long nail and scrape the point across the surface. Develop long, scratch-like streaks randomly across the surface. Add nail hole marks by lightly tapping the nail's point and head into the surface with a hammer.

MASKING AND RULING

The masking and ruling techniques provide clean, crisp lines of color on any surface. When you desire an exact thin line of color, you would use the ruling technique. When you desire a broader band of color, you would use the masking technique. Masking and ruling techniques can be combined for painted effects in varying widths of color. Masking and ruling can be completed on any interior surface as well as furniture. Due to the tedious qualities of both techniques, you'll need a great deal of patience to tackle larger areas. Complementing techniques that work well with masking and ruling—in a room or on furniture—include sponging, decorative design and tortoiseshell.

With ruling, you can make a thin line of color from about 1/16 to 1/8 of an inch. To complete this method, you'll need to become proficient with a tool called a ruling pen. A ruling pen is mainly used by draftsmen and graphic technical illustrators. It can be filled with drawing inks, acrylic, oil or latex paints to create fine line work.

PREPARATION

For the masking technique, use a ruler and pencil to measure the area to be banded with color. First, carefully mark off the area with small dots or dash marks, then connect them with a straight line. Continue this around the entire surface until you have all areas marked. Place the tape just beside the pencil line so you actually paint over the line. On interior bands (bands that do not end on the edge of the surface), mask off both sides. When placing tape

on the surface, wait to rub down the tape until all areas are masked off. This will allow you to make changes if needed.

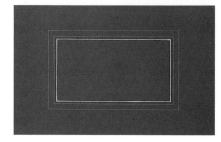

Masking and ruling can be combined or used separately. Masking creates wide bands of color (top); ruling defines an area with fine line work (bottom).

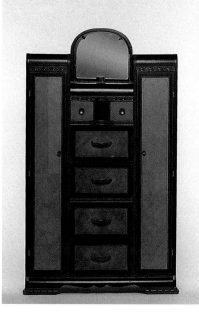

KEYS TO SUCCESS

⸙ Accuracy in measuring and marking off areas is very important to achieve even, consistent, straight lines of color.

⸙ Always work on a clean, sealed surface. A surface such as a semigloss painted surface or varnish surface provides a smooth, semislick area that will accept paint well and can be corrected easily by wiping. A very porous surface will soak up the paint too quickly.

⸙ Be sure to burnish edges of tape that paint will be brushed along. If any areas of the tape are not adhered to the surface, the paint will seep underneath.

⸙ When masking, there is no need to rub down on edges of the tape that will not receive paint. This will aid in removing the tape later.

⸙ When using the ruling pen, if you have difficulty getting the paint to flow, touch the tip of the pen with your finger to draw out the paint.

⸙ To ensure a straight line, run the ruling pen alongside a cork-backed raised ruler. The raised ruler will prevent any paint from seeping under it.

Materials needed:
Acrylic or latex paints (or oil paints or drawing ink)
Water (or paint thinner for oil-based paints)
Sponge brushes, round brush and liner brush
Ruling pen
Large cork-backed raised ruler
White artists' tape
Pencil and eraser
Craft knife
Paper towels and scrap paper

MASKING

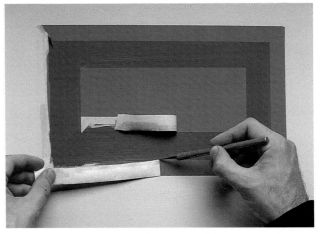

STEP 1. Once all areas are marked and masked off, you can apply paint. A sponge brush provides the smoothest application of color. Always brush parallel to the tape edge, not directly into it. (The latter can cause paint seepage.) Let it dry and apply additional coats until you get an opaque finish. In this example, the base coat was a medium blue. Then areas were masked with white tape, and dark blue was applied to the inner areas and light blue to the outer area (as shown, above right).

STEP 2. When removing the tape, pull up at an angle away from the painted band area. If you have any problems with the paint pulling up unevenly, you can lightly score the paint/tape edge with a craft knife.

RULING

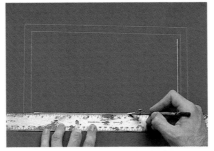

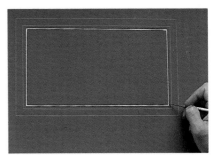

STEP 1. First, you need to load the ruling pen. Fill a round brush with thinned paint, then stroke the brush over the open slot area of the ruling pen. Clean the excess paint off the side of the pen with your fingers or a paper towel. Then turn the screw to tighten the slot opening. Holding the pen at a forty-five degree angle, test how the paint flows by drawing on a sheet of paper.

STEP 2. Now, line up the ruler, hold the pen at a forty-five degree angle, and place the first line on the surface. Complete parallel lines first, then complete intersections and overlays (where lines overlap) with the perpendicular lines. When connecting lines at intersections or at overlays, allow the first line executed to dry fully so it won't smear when you place the ruler over it.

STEP 3. Touch up any obvious stop-and-start areas of the line work by cleaning up around them with a fine liner brush and the background color.

CHAPTER 5. INTERMEDIATE PAINTED FINISH TECHNIQUES

Stenciling
Woodgraining
Strié
Moiré
Gilding
Fantasy Finishes

The intermediate techniques in this chapter will introduce you to more involved methods than those in chapter four. Two of these techniques—woodgraining and moiré—are defined as faux finishes because they duplicate real surfaces. The remaining four techniques—stenciling, strié, gilding and fantasy finishes—are purely decorative.

Take the time to read the instructions and follow along with the photographs. Practice on sample boards before attempting a technique for the first time on your wall or furniture surface. Mastering these six techniques will enable you to design with an elegant, opulent and professional look in your home.

STENCILING

Stenciling is an attractive way to repeat a decorative pattern quickly. It can look just as effective as repeating a pattern freehand, and can be completed in a quarter of the time. Stenciling is traditionally used on walls, but it can be done on drapes, furniture and floors. Many people think of stenciling as a country-style design, but you can use Victorian, contemporary or Southwestern styles, among others. Stenciling is best suited for kitchens, bathrooms and bedrooms. Complementing techniques that work well with stenciling include sponging, ragging and strié.

Stenciling can use several different tools for a slight variation in the final look, but the principles are the same. You'll line up a series of Mylar overlays with tape. The Mylar overlays have shapes cut out of them. You'll apply paint through these openings with a stencil brush, a natural sea sponge, or a can of spray paint.

Stenciling is a quick way to repeat a design on a surface, whether you use a brush (top), a sponge (middle), or a spray can (bottom).

PREPARATION

Use ready-made stencils, or you can design and cut your own. To cut your own stencil, place a sheet of glass over your neatly drawn design. Next, tape a piece of Mylar over the glass. Use a craft knife or stencil cutter to cut out the design. Cut a separate stencil overlay for each section of the design where different colors are within one inch of each other. On each overlay, use a black marker to create center cross lines and draw the parts of the design that you're not cutting out. This will help you line up the pattern as it repeats.

KEYS TO SUCCESS
❧ When loading the stencil brush, apply a small amount of paint to the bristles. Excess paint on the brush causes blotchy markings and paint seepage underneath the Mylar stencil.
❧ The same approach applies when using a sponge as the stencil tool. Load paint sparingly, so as not to create seepage.
❧ When stenciling with the spray paint, it is imperative that you mask out all surrounding areas properly so no paint specks fall where you don't want them.
❧ For intricate stencil designs with many different color overlays, go around the surface with one overlay at a time. For simple designs with one or two overlays, you can complete the whole design in one spot before moving on.

Materials needed:
Acrylic or latex paints
Precut stencils (or, make your own with sheets of clear Mylar, designs, a sheet of glass, craft knife or heated stencil cutter, and permanent medium-line black marker)
Repositionable tape
Stencil brushes in various sizes
Natural sea sponge
Spray paints
Paper towels
Scrap paper

BRUSH STENCILING

STEP 1. Load the tip of the brush with a minimum amount of paint; wipe the excess onto a paper towel. There should be only a faint amount of color on the brush. Hold the brush upright and perpendicular to the surface and, in a light swirling motion, stroke from the edge of the stencil into the center.

STEP 2. If you wish to create contrast in the design, allow the center area to show some of the surface's base color. Darken toward the stencil's edge with more color. Remember, you need a light touch and a minimum amount of paint to prevent paint seepage underneath the stencil.

SPONGE STENCILING

STEP 1. For a more rustic, textured stencil look, apply paint with a sponge. The effect will be rough compared to the stencil brush application, but for some design styles this approach is great. Load the sponge with paint and pat the sponge on a scrap paper surface to remove excess paint.

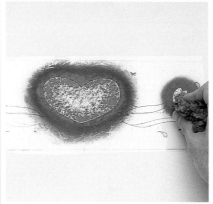

STEP 2. With the stencil taped in position, lightly pat the open areas of the design with the sponge. Heavy paint application will cause paint seepage, so be careful. Allow the first color to dry before applying an overlay of another color.

SPRAY PAINT STENCILING

STEP 1. For yet another look, you can stencil with spray paints. Exercise extreme care when using this tool—you could end up with an array of paint specks where you don't wish to have them. Tape the stencil to the surface, then tape scrap papers all around the stencil.

STEP 2. Hold the spray can about six to eight inches away from the stencil. Using a light, sporadic motion, gently sweep across the stencil. You can achieve a soft misting of color or fill in more solid, opaque colors. You can intermix your coloration or keep the colors separate.

Faux bois, the French term meaning false wood, can be completed in any wood type. Each different kind of woodgrain has a corresponding painted finish technique. A chapter could be developed solely on woodgraining variations. Here, a basic woodgrain is illustrated, one that duplicates a stained heart of pine.

Painted woodgrain allows you to accent and exaggerate patterning of the grain compared to real wood, achieve woodgrain on a previously painted surface without stripping, or reproduce hard-to-find or expensive woods. Woodgraining can be applied to doors, woodwork, paneling, floors and furniture. Complementing techniques that work well with woodgraining include marbleizing, texturizing and ragging.

PREPARATION

It is better to brush on the base coat color than to roll it on. Rollers will leave visible marks that the glaze will pick up. Apply several coats of a tan base until it's opaque. Seal it with several light mistings of clear acrylic spray.

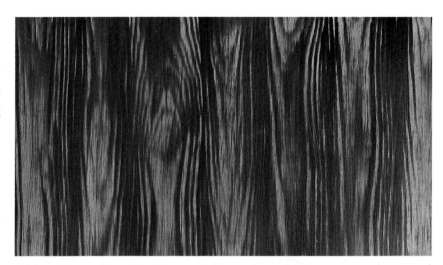

Rich woodgrain (above) can be completed on any surface, creating a realistic wood texture. Here, a stained heart of pine is depicted. Woodgraining can be completed with specially designed woodgrain tools or can be reproduced with the aid of brushes and combing tools. The graining techniques that require woodgraining tools must be completed in oil-based glazes. The glaze must stay wet long enough for you to make your marks into it.

KEYS TO SUCCESS

❧ Heart of pine woodgraining requires the use of oil-based paints and glaze. The glaze must stay wet enough for you to make your marks in it.

❧ Realistic woodgraining depends on proper paint consistency and believable coloration. Mix paints with sufficient painting glaze, and use natural earth tones.

❧ Correct handling of your woodgraining tool is important in creating the marks in the glaze that are to represent the true woodgrain.

❧ When woodgraining a large area, section it off so you work on areas no larger than 3 feet wide at a time.

❧ Begin by brushing an even coat of the color glaze on the surface using a large base coat brush. A minimum amount of brushstrokes in the color glaze is best. Try for a consistent tonal quality to the color application.

Materials needed:
Tan or beige semigloss latex paint; artists' oil color paints in burnt umber, burnt sienna and asphaltum
Large base coat bristle brush
Clear painting glaze
Large mop brush, badger softener brush and liner brush
Woodgrain tool for heart of pine
Pan for mixing paint and glaze
Clear acrylic spray
Paper towels

STEP 1. Create an earth tone color glaze by mixing equal parts of burnt umber, burnt sienna and asphaltum. Add clear painting glaze to the oil color in a pan; mix to a soupy consistency. You want to achieve a thin, semitransparent color glaze. Brush on glaze over the surface with the base coat brush.

STEP 2. Pick up the woodgraining tool and practice the proper rocking rotation to achieve the graining effect. Hold the tool loosely by the handle; rock and rotate the tool as you drag it down the surface in one continuous motion.

STEP 3. Each time you start at the top, begin at a different point on the tool to change the grain markings. Complete this across the area with the wet glaze. Wipe excess color off the tool with a paper towel as needed.

STEP 4. Pick up the badger softener brush and stroke over the surface lightly, following the grain, holding the brush perpendicular to the surface. Blend and soften specific areas with the mop brush. Additional grain markings can be completed with a liner brush loaded with color glaze to accent and highlight.

Woodgrain techniques that require the use of brushes alone, such as mahogany (shown here), can be rendered in water-based paints.

STRIÉ

Strié, simply defined, is a series of irregular streaks in a linear pattern. It was originally an intermediate step in creating some woodgrain types. Today, it is used as an end result. Strié is best suited for walls, but it can be used on sections of furniture as well. Complementing techniques that work well with strié in a room or on a piece of furniture include stenciling, marbleizing and gilding.

You can achieve a strié effect using only a flogger brush to make linear marks. As an option, you can add more texture and a second color with a natural sea sponge. Either technique is effective; it is purely a personal choice.

PREPARATION

Begin by masking with painter's mask-out tape all surrounding areas that will not be receiving the strié finish. Next, apply a base coat color to your surface using a base coat bristle brush. Don't use a roller because it will cause a pebbly texture. You want the base coat to have a brushed appearance. Apply several coats of paint, until you have an opaque coverage.

The linear pattern of the strié technique adds an intriguing texture to wall and furniture surfaces.

KEYS TO SUCCESS

❧ Remember that this is a hand-painted look—there will be imperfections in the linear qualities. Strive for a straight-line effect, but the finished look will not be ruler perfect.

❧ The consistent pressure you apply to the brush is critical to the painted finish. Stroke from the top of the surface to the bottom in one continuous motion without stopping or hesitating.

❧ The strié technique must be completed in oil-based paints to allow enough open time to create the streaked finish.

❧ Choose colors that are not in high contrast to each other. Place a lighter glaze color over a darker base coat or vice versa—the base and glaze can be two different colors or different shades of the same color.

❧ If you choose the optional sponge step, do it directly after completing a section of stroking with the flogger brush.

❧ If you need to stop during the process, try to break at a corner of the room or surface. It is best to always work next to a wet section to prevent any noticeable stop-and-start lines.

Materials needed:
Semigloss oil enamel paints and/or artists' oil color paints
Base coat bristle brush, flogger brush
Clear painting glaze
Natural sea sponge
Large jar
Paint trays
Painter's mask-out tape

STEP 1. Create a color glaze by mixing clear painting glaze with oil paint. Develop a thin, flowing color mixture in a jar, then pour it into a paint tray. Using the base coat brush, apply glaze to the surface from top to bottom in a width of about 8 to 12 inches (about two and a half widths of the flogger brush).

STEP 2. Using the flogger brush, stroke from top to bottom in one continuous motion. Position your brush so it is parallel to the wall, applying a good deal of pressure as you stroke. Cock the handle of the flogger brush slightly toward you to keep the pressure continuous.

STEP 3. (Optional.) Create another color mixture of clear painting glaze plus a second color (lighter or darker than the first color). Once again, develop a thin, flowing color mixture. Dip the natural sea sponge into the new mixture and stroke over the wet glaze on the surface. Stroke from the top of the surface all the way to the bottom.

MOIRÉ

The moiré painted finish duplicates the wavy, watery pattern found on silk moiré fabric. You'll use paint to create the fabric design on any surface you desire. Use the moiré technique when you want a high-style, opulent look. This painted finish is most effective when used in small doses such as in a foyer, above or below a chair rail, or in small rooms. The moiré finish is best suited for wall surfaces and would be out of place on floors and ceilings. Complementing techniques that work well in a room with moiré include glazing, marbleizing and gilding.

The moiré finish is done with oil-based paints and woodgraining tools and combs. The glaze is applied to the surface; then the tools make their marks, which are blended to create the wavy, woodgrain-like pattern.

PREPARATION
Mask out all surrounding areas that will not be receiving the moiré finish with painter's mask-out tape. Next, apply a base coat color to the surface using a large base coat bristle brush. Don't use a roller because it will cause a pebbly texture—you want the base coat to have a brushed appearance. Apply several coats of paint until you have an opaque coverage.

The rich look of the moiré painted finish adds softness to a hard surface in the same way that covering it with silk moiré fabric would.

STEP 1. Create a color glaze by mixing clear painting glaze and oil enamel or artists' oil color in a large jar. Develop a thin, flowing color mixture. Pour it into a paint tray. Brush on an 8-inch width of glaze with the base coat bristle brush. While the glaze is still wet, wipe the surface with a rag in a linear pattern from top to bottom to remove excess color. This step is rather messy, so wear rubber gloves.

STEP 2. Run a woodgraining tool down the surface from top to bottom, rotating and rocking it to create its pattern. Next to the woodgrain marks run a combing tool down the surface, then repeat the woodgraining tool again. Create markings on the 8-inch section of wet color glaze.

STEP 3. Quickly pick up the bristle softener brush and stroke across the markings toward the right, blurring the pattern slightly. This will create the watered, wavy pattern of the silk moiré fabric. Repeat the above steps as you work around the surface. Remember to vary the tool markings.

KEYS TO SUCCESS

❧ The color value of the glaze in which you make the moiré markings is critical. For a successful, realistic moiré, the glaze applied on top of the base coat is only slightly lighter than the base.

❧ Very little paint is used in the color glaze to duplicate the subtle effect of light catching the wavy patterning of the silk.

❧ When applying the color glaze to the surface, stroke from top to bottom in sections approximately 8 inches wide. Each new section of wet glaze should be just wide enough for you to run three rows of markings.

❧ Alternate and vary the patterning of the tools. For example: Stroke with the woodgrain tool twice in a row, then stroke with the comb, follow with the woodgrain tool, then the comb. Don't make marks with one tool more than twice in a row.

Materials needed:
Semigloss oil enamel paints and/or artists' oil color paints
Large base coat bristle brush, bristle softener brush
Clear painting glaze
Woodgraining tool
Combing tools
Large jar
Paint trays
Painter's mask-out tape
Cotton rags
Rubber gloves

Gold and silver leaf add sophistication to almost any decorative surface, whether it's furniture or accessories. Their shimmery qualities add an air of elegance to your work. Although gold and silver leaf are often used as a border or trim element of other finishes, they can stand alone as a singular statement.

Gilding can be completed in two ways: an opaque method where the leaf sheets are applied overlapping each other, or an antique look where cracks are purposely developed between the sheets during the application process. With either approach, an attractive, eye-catching look is the result.

Gilding is most effective used in small doses on sections of furniture, accessories or architectural accents such as chair rails, cornices, dados, columns or corbels. When placing gold or silver leaf in large amounts, the interior space must be significant to handle the high level of dramatic and intense qualities gilding provides. Only high-style rooms such as dining and living rooms or places where a dramatic look is desired should be gilded. Complementing techniques that work well with gilding in a room or on a furniture surface include marbleizing, strié and moiré.

Preparation
Take your time in preparing the surface, making sure it is smooth, clean and sealed. Next, base coat the area to be leafed with a mid- to dark-value paint.

A dark base tone provides a stronger contrast to leafed areas than a light background does.

Leaf sizing is the adhesive to which the leaf will stick. Stir it thoroughly but gently, so as not to form bubbles. Using a small round brush for border areas or large sponge brush for background areas, apply an even, smooth coat of sizing to the appropriate parts of the surface. If any sizing drips elsewhere, quickly clean the area with a cotton ball or swab dipped in turpentine. Let it set up according to the sizing label's instructions (one to eight hours). Once it becomes tacky, you will have three to four hours to work on it before it dries too hard to accept leaves.

Tear a stack of leaves into smaller, manageable pieces, leaving the tissue overlay intact. For best results, tear the sheets against the edge of a ruler.

STEP 1. Pick up a single piece of leaf (hold it by the tissue at the top and brush at the bottom). Put it in place on your surface quickly to avoid wrinkles. Lightly brush over the tissue with a soft-haired brush to smooth and secure the leaf. As you do this, the tissue will peel away from the leaf. Be careful not to brush the tissue into the sizing.

This bread crumb tray was gilded with a solid application for a bright and bold look.

STEP 2. Fill the entire area you've sized in this manner. As you place down the leaf pieces, you can leave cracks of the base coat showing through for a worn, antique look, or you can overlap the pieces so no color remains. If you overlap the pieces, don't try to tear off the excess until the sizing is thoroughly dry. (Allow at least twelve hours; twenty-four hours is best.)

STEP 3. When dry, remove any excess leaf by using a soft-haired brush to burnish or lightly brush it off the surface. Don't use heavy pressure. Brush excess leaf scraps into a box and save them to use as fill-in pieces on your next leaf job.

STEP 4. Buff the surface very lightly with a clean cotton rag to remove any small fringes of leaf that you've missed. Brush or spray on a coat of varnish to seal your surface. Don't handle the leafed areas before varnishing because your fingers will leave marks.

Gilding also can be applied to create an antique, worn effect.

KEYS TO SUCCESS

❧ Proper preparation of the surface to be leafed is crucial to the gilding technique. Any bumps and valleys in the surface are magnified once gilded.

❧ Handle the leaf sheets carefully. Don't touch them with your fingers—the oils from your hands will tarnish and mark the suface.

❧ Although you can use real gold and silver leaf, most times the less expensive choice is imitation leaf. Gold and silver leaf come in books or packages of twenty-five 5½-inch square tissue-covered sheets.

❧ Allow ample time for the leaf sizing to set up, and then for it to dry, for proper leaf adhesion.

❧ Remember that each sheet is very lightweight and the slightest breeze can send it soaring. Therefore, work in an area free of heavy air circulation.

Materials needed:
Paints: base coat color of mid- to dark-value latex or enamel (black was used here)
No. 3 round brush, large sponge brush, soft-haired brush (sable flat or mop brush)
Leaf sizing (quick or slow dry)
Turpentine
Cotton balls or swabs
Cardboard box
Ruler
Cotton rags
Varnish and varnish brush
Gold or silver leaf

Fantasy finishes are in the realm of vivid imagination and illusion. Fantasy finishes are make-believe like faux finishes, but they take this falsehood one step further. Fantasy-style painted marbles, woodgrains and stone surfaces exaggerate the true patterning and are created in nonrealistic color schemes. With this technique, it is not the intention to fool the viewer into believing he or she is looking at the real thing. Fantasy finishes are what I call "designer" painted finishes because their main purpose is to coordinate in color and texture with fabrics, wallpapers and accessories. Examples of fantasy finishes would include a black and gold marble surface, or a blue/green woodgrain, both of which are presented later.

Fantasy finishes can work in any type of room or on any furniture surface. Complementing techniques that work well with fantasy finishes include subtle finishes such as glazing, masking or ruling, and sponging.

PREPARATION

Base coat your surface with one of the colors in the color scheme of your fantasy finish. Apply several coats, until you get an opaque coverage. Create painting glazes by mixing oil colors with clear painting glaze to the desired consistency. (The consistency you want will depend on the painting technique being used.) Add a few drops of cobalt siccative drier to aid in the drying process.

Let your imagination run wild to create a fantasy finish like this one. Rich, black marbleizing techniques were combined with gold to create a designer marble effect. (See chapter six for in-depth instructions for creating realistic marbleizing effects.)

KEYS TO SUCCESS

❧ Determine the color scheme of the area you're decorating with the fantasy finish. What are the dominant color, secondary color and accent colors?

❧ Coordinate wallpaper and fabrics near your fantasy finish. If the area has a busy pattern already, play down the painted finish's pattern. If the area lacks pattern, exaggerate the pattern in the painted finish.

❧ Few things can go wrong when creating fantasy finishes, since you are not out to copy a specific surface. Follow the basic painting techniques in this book but feel free to play up either the color *or* texture of any of the painted finish techniques (but not both).

❧ Just because you're creating a fantasy finish does not mean you should pick garish colors or odd color combinations. Be tasteful in color, and you'll achieve better results.

Materials needed:
Artists' oil color or acrylic color paints
Base coat bristle brush, bristle softener brush, badger softener brush, mop brush, liner brush
Painting medium—turpentine or water
Clear painting glaze
Palette and palette knife
Cobalt siccative drier
Feathers or woodgraining tools
Cotton rags
Toothbrush

Black and Gold Marble

STEP 1. Base coat with black enamel. Apply an overall black glaze, rag over it and brush lightly with a badger softener brush. Create "ghost" areas of gold metallic oil color with a feather and blend with a bristle softener brush. With the tip of a feather, use a thin-consistency gold to establish primary veins.

STEP 2. Cut back the veins by ragging over them lightly. Blend with the badger softener brush. Develop secondary veins coming off the main veins, and add a few veins independent of them. Blend these with the badger softener brush. Add gold flyspecks with thin-consistency paint and a toothbrush.

Green and Blue Woodgrain

STEP 1. Base coat the surface with a cream-colored enamel. Apply a green glaze to a section of the surface with a base coat bristle brush. Right next to this, add an area of blue glaze. Blend with the bristle softener brush where the two colors meet—just enough to break up the division lines between colors, not enough to lose the two distinct colors.

STEP 2. Run a woodgraining tool over the surface, rocking it as you go along. Start at a new place on the tool for each strip of graining. Complete this over the area where glaze is applied. Soften the grain marks overall with the badger softener brush as shown. Complete specific area blending with the mop brush. Add desired detail grain marks with color and a liner brush.

CHAPTER 6. MARBLEIZING

Black Marbleizing
Green Serpentine
Marbleizing
White Alabaster Marbleizing
Brecciated Marbleizing

These four faux marbleizing finishes create magic on just about any surface. The rich color tones of the painted marble enhance tabletops, columns and floors. Experiment with these marbleizing techniques after you have become accustomed to some of the easy and intermediate painted finish techniques.

Follow my step-by-step techniques for creating a marble effect, but don't be afraid to alter the look of the marble. A faux finish is meant to initially fool the eye into believing it sees a marble surface, only to realize it is a painted effect. Feel free to exaggerate the patterns of the marble to create a theatrical look on furniture, walls or floor surfaces. Combine several marble types on a furniture or floor surface for an inlaid tile effect.

BLACK MARBLEIZING

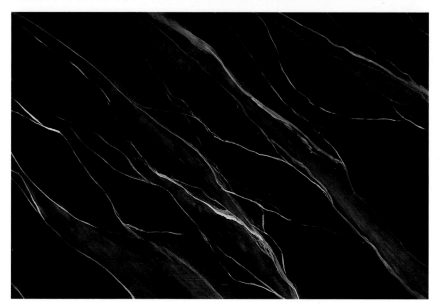

The black-and-white contrast creates an eye-catching marble pattern for many surfaces. Black marbleizing is a great technique for a beginner to experiment with.

The black marbleizing technique creates a rich, dramatic look with its high contrast of black background and white veining. This type of marble is an excellent choice to experiment with if you have never marbleized before. The black marble technique is easy to achieve and will introduce you to the basic principles of marbleizing. In all types of marbleizing, there is a constant add-and-subtract process as you try to duplicate with paint the real marble's layers that are created over years of built-up mineral deposits.

Black marbleizing is best suited for a dark, dramatic effect in a room or on a piece of furniture. You can use this technique on many surfaces, including walls, floors, ceilings and furniture. On large areas, break up the space into sections like tiles to create the realistic illusion. Complementing techniques that work well with black marbleizing include gilding, other marbles and woodgraining.

PREPARATION

Use a sponge brush to base your surface with several coats of black enamel paint. Next, create a black glaze by mixing black oil color with the clear painting glaze. Create a thin, soupy consistency glaze to which you'll add a few drops of cobalt siccative drier.

KEYS TO SUCCESS

❧ For black marbleizing, proper paint consistency and drying are crucial. During the painting process—with the aid of a paint drier product—the surface will become tacky, which will help create the blurred qualities to the marble effect.

❧ Always cut back color after applying by patting the surface with a rag wadded in your hand.

❧ You must properly develop the vein structure to provide the illusion of marble. In most marbles, there are primary (large) veins and secondary (smaller) veins. The primary veins are placed on the surface first; then some secondary veins work off the primary veins, while others are independent of the primaries.

❧ Always paint the veins at a diagonal to the surface.

❧ When placing the ghost areas on the black marble, apply a few large areas of white, varying their size from wide to thin.

❧ Each piece of the same type of black marble should have varying amounts of vein markings—no two are alike. This example has an "average" number of veins. You can add or subtract for a totally different look. Don't overdo it and place too many veins on one area of the surface. If you lose too much of your veining in the blending process, simply restroke and blend lightly.

Materials needed:
Black oil enamel paint, artists' oil color paints in lamp black, titanium white
Bristle softener brush, badger softener brush, large mop brush, liner brush, base coat bristle brush, sponge brush
Clear painting glaze
Cobalt siccative drier
Cotton rags
Fine-pointed chicken feathers

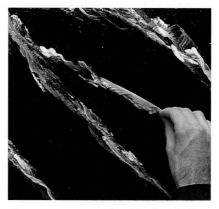

STEP 1. Using the base coat bristle brush, apply the black glaze over the surface. It is not necessary to coat the entire surface with the black oil color glaze, but cover at least 75 percent of the surface. Next, pat over the surface with a rag (as shown), and then brush in a crisscross motion with the bristle softener brush to smooth and spread the paint glaze.

STEP 2. Begin to develop the black marble's ghost areas—those blurred white shapes that the veins travel along. Using a feather, stroke on white that has been thinned with paint glaze to a soupy consistency. The shapes should resemble a river in that they flow in varying widths.

STEP 3. Crumple a rag in your hand and pat the white ghost areas to soften them. Now, pick up the bristle softener brush and stroke over the white to blend and blur it into the black. Stroke in the same direction as the white markings; do not stroke across the markings. At this point, the paint should develop a tacky quality because of the cobalt siccative drier.

STEP 4. Load the feather with white oil color that has been thinned with painting glaze to a flowing consistency. Hold the feather loosely in your hand and make light, quick strokes with the feather's tip across the surface. Allow the primary veins to be large at certain points and taper to narrower widths.

STEP 5. Lightly cut back the veins by patting the surface with the rag. This will remove excess paint. Now, pick up the badger softener brush and blend by gently brushing along the veins to set the paint into the surface. Always brush in the same direction in which the veins flow. The vein work should not look as if it is resting on top of the surface.

STEP 6. Add secondary veins by loading the feather or a liner brush with thinned white paint and stroke it on the surface. Use a light touch to create thin, delicate veins. Add to the surface a few independent secondary veins flowing near the primary veins. Cut back the secondary veins with the badger softener brush or mop brush.

Green Serpentine Marbleizing

The green serpentine style of marbleizing is one of the most popular as well as one of the most dramatic used in decorating circles. The serpentine marble's green-to-black spotted markings provide a unique textural quality that catches the eye. Just as real serpentine marble is made up of layers of minerals, the faux painted finish is made up of layers of paint. The secret behind the realistic look is to soften and blend away the texture as you build it up.

The green serpentine marble is ideal for use on tabletops, tile shapes on floors, or sections of walls such as below a chair rail. This marble type is elegant in a foyer, a den or library, or a dining room. Complementing techniques that work well with green serpentine marbleizing include white alabaster marbleizing, gilding and strié.

Preparation

Base coat the surface to be marbleized with black enamel. Apply several coats until it's opaque. Next, create a color glaze by mixing lamp black oil color and clear painting glaze until you achieve a soupy, flowing consistency. Add a few drops of cobalt siccative drier. Apply the glaze liberally to the surface using the base coat bristle brush. Spread out the color glaze evenly by ragging with a cotton rag and brushing with the bristle softener brush.

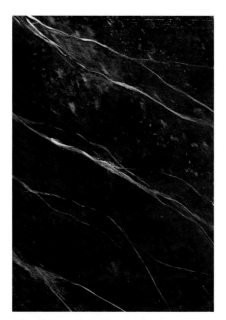

The deep, rich coloration and texture of the green serpentine marble (shown at right completed on a tabletop) make it one of the most popular choices when marbleizing interior and furniture surfaces.

Keys to Success

❧ Creating realistic serpentine marbleizing depends on proper paint consistency and drying, proper vein markings, and development of primary and secondary veins.

❧ You must properly develop the vein structure to provide the illusion of marble. In most marbles, there are primary (large) veins and secondary (smaller) veins. The primary veins are placed on the surface first; then some secondary veins work off the primary veins, while others are independent of the primaries.

❧ Veins can start and stop on the surface; they needn't continue off it as long as they trail off until they are invisible.

❧ The veins should be placed on a diagonal in relationship to how the surface will be viewed.

❧ If you lose too much of the vein structure during the blending process, add more color and blend with a lighter touch.

Materials needed:
Black oil enamel paint; artists' oil color paints in leaf green dark, Prussian blue, ultramarine blue, titanium white, viridian, permanent green light, lamp black
Bristle softener brush, badger softener brush, large mop brush, liner or scroll brush, base coat bristle brush, sponge brush
Clear painting glaze
Cobalt siccative drier
Cotton rags
Natural sea sponge
Fine-pointed chicken feathers
Palette

STEP 1. Using the base coat bristle brush, apply random splotches of leaf green dark, viridian, and permanent green light that have been thinned with painting glaze. Without cleaning the brush, mix together on your palette a touch of Prussian blue, ultramarine blue and lamp black. Add this dark color to the surface in a few places.

STEP 2. To add depth, cut back the colors by patting the surface with a rag crumpled up in your hand. Blend your colors into the base glaze mixture by lightly dusting the surface with the bristle softener brush. Hold the brush perpendicular to the surface and dust over the paint in a crisscross motion.

STEP 3. To add texture and color, randomly sponge on leaf green dark, permanent green light and viridian, all of which have been thinned with painting glaze. Sponge all over in no specific direction or pattern. Use a rag to cut back the color and markings. Dust over the colors with the bristle softener brush to subtly blend the paint.

STEP 4. To develop the first layer of primary veins, dip the feather into titanium white that's been thinned with clear painting glaze to the consistency of whipped cream. Stroke the feather diagonally over the surface, creating a ragged line. Develop the vein pattern by establishing these large main veins as well as small, secondary ones.

STEP 5. The veins are now sitting on top of your surface. To make them look as if they're embedded, cut them back and soften them into the colors underneath by patting them with a rag and a mop brush as shown. Lightly brush over the entire surface with the bristle softener brush to set the veins and colors into the surface once more.

STEP 6. One of the last steps is to accent the veins with more white and add smaller secondary veins as needed, using the tip of the feather or a liner or scroll brush. Soften with the badger softener brush to set these final veins into the surface, always brushing along the same direction as each vein.

WHITE ALABASTER MARBLEIZING

The white alabaster marble is one of the softest, most attractive marbles around. It is a translucent, tinted white ranging from pale gray to pinkish gray. Its vein markings are not as evident as in other marbles, but are more blurred in coloration. The white alabaster marble is ideal for floors, tabletops, columns, foyers, living rooms and dining rooms. White alabaster marble is a complement to other marbles when designing with a multiple tile layout on floors or creating inlaid shapes of two marble types. Complementing techniques that work well with the white alabaster marbleizing technique include gilding, strié and other marble types.

PREPARATION

Base the surface to be marbleized with white enamel; apply several coats until it's opaque. Create a white glaze by mixing titanium white with clear painting glaze to a soupy consistency. Add a few drops of cobalt siccative drier to the glaze mixture. Brush on the white glaze over the surface with the base coat bristle brush. It is not necessary to cover the entire surface with the white glaze. Rag the surface with a crumpled rag and brush over it lightly with a bristle softener brush.

The markings of the white alabaster marble are extremely subtle. The veining is blurred, appearing to be embedded underneath the surface.

KEYS TO SUCCESS
❧ To create realistic white alabaster marble, you must develop the depth of the layers of coloration.

❧ Proper paint consistency and drying, correct vein markings, and development of vein structures that appear to have depth will make the white alabaster marble look real.

❧ Thin all the oil colors with painting glaze to a thin, creamy consistency.

❧ Blend smoothly by brushing over the entire surface with the badger softener brush. This should remove any obvious brushstroke marks, and blend and blur the coloration below.

❧ A transparent glaze over the dried paint finish will create depth to the marble by setting back the marking colorations on the surface. If you want, you can repeat the final steps of varnishing and glazing multiple times.

Materials needed:
Artists' oil color paints in titanium white, raw umber, Payne's gray, lamp black, burnt alizarin (optional)
Base coat bristle brush, bristle softener brush, badger softener brush, mop brush, spalter brush
Clear painting glaze
Cobalt siccative drier
Cotton rags
Fine-pointed chicken feathers
White oil enamel
Oil-based polyurethane varnish

STEP 1. Pick up raw umber on the side of a feather and stroke diagonally over the surface to begin developing the markings. These are not thin veins; they are more like fuzzy lines of color. Next, rag over the markings to soften them. Brush over the surface with the bristle softener brush to make the markings blur into the white base.

STEP 2. Pick up touches of Payne's gray and lamp black on the end of the feather and dab here and there over the surface to create subtle, irregular dashes of color. Rag over the surface and blend with the bristle softener brush. You can blend specific areas with the mop brush, if needed.

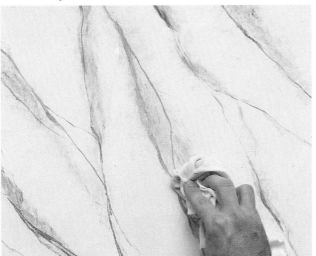

STEP 3. Adding small hints of a pinkish cast is an option. Pick up a touch of burnt alizarin on a feather and dab a little here and there. Knock back the colors with a rag and soften with the bristle softener brush. Allow the surface to dry thoroughly. Use the spalter brush to coat with varnish.

STEP 4. Add titanium white and a touch of raw umber to a clear painting glaze. Mix to create a transparent glaze. Brush this over the surface with the spalter brush. It is important not to allow any visible brush marks to show. If needed, rag over the surface and blend with the badger softener brush.

Brecciated Marbleizing

Breccia is a rock composed of sharp, angled fragments embedded in a fine-grained substance such as sand or clay. The brecciated marble that is made up of this dramatic, active pattern is very attractive when used in small doses on furniture tops, columns and tile shapes. Use less pattern-oriented marbles such as white alabaster with the brecciated marble when designing with a multiple tile layout on floors or creating inlaid shapes of two marble types. The brecciated marble is effective in rooms where high drama is desired; it creates an elegant flair to many surfaces. Complementing techniques that work well with the brecciated marbleizing technique in a room or on furniture surfaces include white alabaster marbleizing, gilding and moiré.

Preparation

Base the surface to be marbleized with white enamel; apply several coats until it's opaque. Now, create a white glaze by mixing titanium white with clear painting glaze to a soupy consistency. Add a few drops of cobalt siccative drier to the glaze mixture. Next, brush on the white glaze over the surface with the base coat bristle brush. It is not necessary to cover the entire surface with the white glaze. Rag the surface with a crumpled rag and brush over lightly with a bristle softener brush. Thin all the other oil colors with clear painting glaze to a thin, creamy consistency. Mix a soft, light pink color

Brecciated marble, although pattern-intensive, is attractive when used in small doses or in sections of a surface. Ideal for tabletops, brecciated marble can also be placed on architectural details.

by adding a touch of burnt alizarin to titanium white. To create the vein structures, you'll need to create a medium-value pink mixture of burnt alizarin plus titanium white and a medium-value mixture of Payne's gray plus titanium white. Add more painting glaze to these two mixtures until you achieve a thin, flowing consistency.

Keys to Success

❧ Attractive brecciated marble is created by developing angled fragments that "float" below the surface. These shapes need to look organic and natural in form to look realistic.

❧ The vein structure works around these shapes in the same flow. The veins can outline the shapes somewhat but don't have to always run up against a floating shape.

❧ Proper paint consistency is essential in creating the brecciated marbleizing.

❧ Don't overwork the patterning of the brecciated marble; you don't want too many fragment structures to develop.

❧ You'll need to cut back the vein and fragment structures by ragging and blending—you don't want the veins and fragment structures to look as if they rest on the surface.

Materials needed:
Artists' oil color paints in titanium white, Payne's gray, burnt alizarin and lamp black
White oil enamel
Base coat bristle brush, bristle softener brush, liner or scroll brush, badger softener brush, spalter brush
Clear painting glaze
Cobalt siccative drier
Cotton rags
Fine-pointed chicken feathers
Natural sea sponge
Old toothbrush
Oil-based polyurethane varnish

STEP 1. Pick up the light pink mixture on the side of the feather, and begin to develop long, irregular floating shapes in the marble surface. These shapes should be staggered on the surface, at a diagonal, in sizes ranging from small to large.

STEP 2. Next, add texture to these shapes by sponging on the pink mixture plus burnt alizarin. Sponge directly over the areas you just painted with the feather. Then, rag over these shapes and blend them gently with the bristle softener brush. You want to lightly blur the shapes and texture marks into the base.

STEP 3. Using another feather loaded with the gray mixture, add in a few veins following the same pattern. Rag over the surface lightly to cut back the veins and then soften with the bristle softener brush. Add in secondary veins using the liner brush or feather's tip; branch most off the primary veins, with a few running independent of the primary veins. Brush over these veins lightly with the badger softener brush.

STEP 4. To add an element of texture, load a toothbrush with thin-consistency, medium-value gray and flyspeck all over the surface, placing stronger amounts of color in white areas. Brush over the flyspecking with the badger softener brush to blur these markings.

STEP 5. If, at this point, the marble pattern is too defined and it looks as if the elements sit on top of the surface, you'll need to glaze over it. Once you're satisfied with the marble pattern, proceed with the finishing techniques. Let the paint thoroughly dry, and varnish it. Cut back the pattern using a spalter brush with a transparent glaze of titanium white plus a touch of Payne's gray. Don't let brush marks show—rag over the surface and/or blend with a badger softener brush if necessary.

CHAPTER 7. ADVANCED PAINTED FINISH TECHNIQUES

Tortoiseshell
Malachite
Trompe l'oeil

The advanced techniques in this chapter provide you with the knowledge to create sophisticated painted finishes and designs on a wide variety of surfaces. These techniques are designed to create realistic imitations of other surfaces. Now that you have mastered the basic and intermediate finishes, you're ready to begin experimenting with these more involved methods.

TORTOISESHELL

Tortoiseshell is a colorful, opulent finish that mimics its namesake. The mottled, translucent, brownish pattern creates a dramatic look when used sparingly. Real tortoiseshell would not be found in large expanses, so when painting faux tortoiseshell you should keep the painted area to a minimum to make it realistic. Tortoiseshell is best suited for small sections of furniture or accessories in rooms such as libraries and dens or any room that is being decorated in natural earth tones. Since the tortoiseshell is so pattern-intensive, it should be coordinated with less pattern-oriented techniques. Complementing techniques that work well with tortoiseshell include gilding, glazing and masking or ruling.

PREPARATION

Begin by sealing the surface to be painted. Base coat the surface with several coats of black enamel, then let it dry. The black base coat acts like a backing material—it strengthens the gold leaf's intensity. Use a sponge brush to coat the surface with gold leaf sizing. Let it dry according to the manufacturer's instructions. Apply the gold leaf to the entire surface, taking care not to wrinkle or tarnish the leaf with too much handling. The gold leaf will show through some of the transparent areas of the tortoiseshell, adding to its richness. (For more information on gilding, see pages 48-49.) Give the leaf and siz-

The translucent, mottled finish of the tortoiseshell is a rich look for small areas of furniture or accessories.

ing twenty-four hours to dry and adhere to the surface, then burnish or rub over it gently to remove excess leaf with a soft, sable-haired brush. After buffing the surface, seal it with a coat of varnish using a natural bristle varnish brush, and let it dry.

Next, place small piles of yellow ochre, burnt sienna, burnt umber and asphaltum on your palette, and add enough clear painting glaze to each to reach a creamy consistency. Add a few drops of cobalt siccative drier to the colors; mix with a palette knife.

STEP 1. After you paint, leaf and varnish the surface (see "Preparation"), use your sponge brush to apply a coat of clear painting glaze. Allow the glaze to set a couple of minutes to begin to get tacky. Using the round brush, dab on diagonal circular shapes of yellow ochre.

STEP 2. Next, add burnt sienna in irregular shapes on the same diagonal using the round brush. Wipe the brush on a paper towel and add shapes of asphaltum and burnt umber. Allow the burnt umber shapes to dominate in size and quantity. Also, allow the gold leaf to show through in some areas.

KEYS TO SUCCESS

❧ For a realistic tortoiseshell finish, limit the area to be painted. Real tortoiseshell would not be found in large expanses.

❧ It is important to develop a diagonal pattern to the color application. When painting the tortoiseshell, the blending and blurring of the paint pattern will make or break the look.

❧ Allow the paints to become slightly tacky for a blurred effect.

Materials needed:
Artists' oil color paints in yellow ochre, burnt sienna, burnt umber and asphaltum; black oil enamel; metallic gold (optional)
Sponge brush, number 3 round brush, soft mop brush, badger softener brush, base coat bristle brush
Gold leaf sizing and gold leaf
Clear painting glaze
Cobalt siccative drier
Old toothbrush
Turpentine
Oil-based polyurethane gloss varnish
Palette and palette knife
Paper towels

An elegant fire screen spotlights framework painted with the black marbleizing technique, and inner panels of tortoiseshell with gold leaf bands. Ruling was completed in gold and black.

STEP 3. Now, use a soft mop brush or badger softener brush to brush over the surface at the same diagonal to pull and blur colors together. The base of clear painting glaze on the surface will aid in the blending/blurring process.

STEP 4. To create texture, flyspeck the surface. Load an old toothbrush and flyspeck with turpentine. The turpentine will cause a reaction to the paints and painting glaze, causing areas to separate like oil separates from vinegar.

STEP 5. Next, flyspeck with thinned burnt umber. Finish with thinned burnt sienna flyspecks. You can also add gold paint flyspecks for a "decorator" look, but if you want the tortoiseshell to look real, skip this color.

MALACHITE

Malachite is a rare mineral carbonate of copper, with variegated colors of green to nearly black. It is pattern-intensive, with wavy streaks of color forming incomplete circles. The technique is a process of adding and subtracting color; color is applied and then removed, thus forming the streaks of paint on the surface. Malachite should be applied only to small accessories such as boxes, lamp bases, sections of columns and small tabletops; and used as a border element in sections of furniture to look like it's inlaid. Complementing techniques that work well with malachite include gilding, glazing, and masking or ruling.

(Above.) The wavy, curving pattern of malachite is exciting to place on small surfaces such as boxes, tabletops and inlaid areas. Avoid large areas of malachite because of its busy design.

PREPARATION

Base the surface to receive the malachite finish with a light emerald green enamel; apply several coats until it's opaque. Now, create the following color mixtures: viridian plus clear painting glaze, viridian plus a small amount of raw umber plus painting glaze, and viridian plus ultramarine blue plus painting glaze. Mix all paint piles to a thin, creamy consistency, to which you add a few drops of cobalt siccative drier. To create tools to make the marks in the glaze, tear corrugated cardboard into pieces of varying widths, all of which have ragged edges. (Tear the top sheet off the cardboard to expose the wavelike pattern between the two outer sheets.)

KEYS TO SUCCESS

❧ To create the pattern of malachite, remove the paint by stroking over the wet paint surface with cardboard. The development of wavy, curved half-circle strokes that overlap one another is crucial to creating believable malachite.

❧ Your design should be abstract, not a specific repeating pattern.

❧ When softening the pattern of the malachite, use an extremely light touch. Don't blur the marks in the glaze.

Materials needed:
Artists' oil color paints in viridian, raw umber, ultramarine blue; light emerald green enamel
Base coat bristle brush, badger softener brush
Stylus or brush handle
Cotton rags
Clear painting glaze
Cobalt siccative drier
Scraps of corrugated cardboard

(Left.) The classic decorative accessory, this obelisk has been finished with a malachite base and a gilded trim.

STEP 1. Place the three color mixtures on the surface one at a time. Stroke in a crisscross motion, overlapping each color with the previous color(s). Apply 50 percent more of the viridian painting glaze mixture than the other colors. Rag over the wet paint with a rag crumpled in your hand. Soften the surface with the badger softener brush.

STEP 2. Use consistent pressure on the edge of the torn cardboard to form wavy, half-circle strokes. Overlap each series of markings, creating a pattern like real malachite stone.

STEP 3. Use a stylus or brush handle tip to scratch a line into the paint following the contour of the larger wavy, half-circle markings.

STEP 4. Soften the pattern slightly by stroking over the surface with the badger softener brush. Just barely touch the surface, as if you are dusting it with a feather duster.

Trompe l'oeil

From painted mural to faux finishes, painted illusion is a popular decorating trend. With trompe l'oeil (pronounced "tromp loi") painting, which means "fool the eye" in French, you can create an almost-photographic realism. For instance, with just a little paint you can fool almost anyone into believing there's a "newly built" shelf over your kitchen stove or deck of cards on a coffee table. Even dimensional-looking wood paneling can be painted on a flat piece of drywall.

In fact, one of the primary benefits to learning trompe l'oeil techniques is saving money. If you can't afford to replace or add real wood paneling or a marble floor to your home, just paint them on. Painted architectural accents such as a wall panel, chair rail, cornice, archway, dado or column can add the illusion of greater depth, space and elegance to your home, and you only have to invest in paint and brushes.

Before you dig into painting a trompe l'oeil project, you need to understand that the deception you get with this technique is momentary. You've created a surprise for the viewer, but the astonishment can only last as long as the admirer remains at the same viewing point as the painting's horizon. For example, if your painting is meant to be viewed while you're standing up, the illusion will be discovered once you sit down.

Preparation

Seal the surface thoroughly before beginning to paint. (See pages 10-19.) A sealed surface will prevent your paint from penetrating the surface and allow you to blend and shade freely. Whether you choose to work in artists' oil or acrylic colors, you should work with the colors as they come from the tube, with a minimum amount of thinning. Only when you add glazing techniques, toward the painting's completion, should you thin the paint significantly with its corresponding medium.

Sketch your design on paper first, to plan the structure and form. Be sure to draw the objects from the viewpoint from which they will be seen most often. Transfer your drawing onto the surface with graphite paper.

Establish a general color scheme for the painting and make notes on your sketch. A quick, colored pencil sketch can be a helpful reference to follow during the painting process. This will also aid in achieving a painting whose colors are harmonious. Set up two palettes— one for acrylics and another for oils. Whip colors with a palette knife with just a few drops of corresponding medium.

Keys to Success

❧ Effective trompe l'oeil tricks the eye into believing it is viewing three-dimensional objects rather than a two-dimensional surface. To achieve this result, the number one principle is to paint all objects at life-sized proportions.

❧ Trompe l'oeil painting must fit into its setting to be believable. Avoid painting any objects that move (humans, animals, bugs).

❧ When attempting a trompe l'oeil for the first time, limit the project to a simple design such as panel molding or a flat object representation.

❧ The viewer of trompe l'oeil should not be aware of your painting techniques. The painted surface should not have visible brushstrokes or paint texture.

❧ If you work from a still life, you may choose to take a photograph for reference. A black-and-white photo will help you see the different values in the items you paint.

❧ Use as large a brush as you feel comfortable with for the area or objects you paint.

Materials needed:
Artists' oil paints in a full spectrum to coordinate with the subject matter being painted; artists' burnt umber acrylic paint
An assortment of red sable and synthetic brushes, such as numbers 8, 12 and 20 flats; numbers 1 and 3 rounds; liner and mop brushes
Two palettes and palette knife
Turpentine and water
Drawing paper and graphite paper
Pencils and colored pencils
Varnish
Clear painting glaze

STEP 1. Begin by developing an underpainting. Outline each object in your design with burnt umber acrylic and a liner brush. Next, establish the tonal range of the entire painting by placing in the light, medium and dark values of each object with the burnt umber on a large, flat brush. Be sure to establish the corresponding shadows that will develop the illusion of dimension. Let this dry for one hour before going on.

Trompe l'oeil painting techniques take a great deal of patience and expertise. You'll need to observe real life and then do your best to imitate it.

STEP 2. Starting with the background and moving forward, block in the colors with oil paints. First, apply the midtones, then the dark tones, and finish with the light tones on each object, as shown. Develop the entire painting instead of working on just one object at a time. This will create harmony in color and in your painting technique. Make any major changes at this time.

STEP 3. Begin to render and shade each object. You want to achieve a smooth color transition from dark to midtone to light tones. Start by completing an initial blending using a flat brush. Move one color into another with choppy crisscross strokes to break division lines. Go over this initial blending with a lighter touch, using the flat and mop brushes (mop brush shown here).

STEP 4. Accent the highlight areas with stronger amounts of white and white plus color, especially in the painting's center of focus. To create the feeling of reality and dimension, exaggerate shadow areas with deep tones placed in the darkest part of the shadow—nearest to the object. This thin area of shadow is almost an outline next to each object. Let this dry, and varnish. Glaze over any areas that need to be set back with a transparent color glaze of oil color plus clear painting glaze.

CHAPTER 8. DECORATIVE PAINTING

Basic Decorative Design
Flowers and Leaves
Fruits and Leaves
Using Fabric and Wallpaper

Decorative painting is an attractive addition to furniture and accessory pieces for your home. But decorative painting can also lend itself to embellishing floors, walls and ceilings. Take the time to practice the basic brushstrokes, for they are the foundation of all types of decorative painting. The basic brushstrokes will lay the groundwork for you to gain brush control and confidence in your paints and tools. Once you have mastered the brushstrokes, you can go on to painting any type of subject. Fruit and flower themes are the most popular in decorative designs. These subjects lend themselves well to any surface as well as fitting into any type of room environment. After you familiarize yourself with the techniques of fruit and flower painting, you can begin to design your own patterns to coordinate with fabric and wallpaper patterns. If you are timid about designing your own patterns, try some of the pattern designs displayed on pages 84-93.

BASIC DECORATIVE DESIGN

Decorative painting, loosely defined, is an ornamentational art form used to decorate functional as well as nonfunctional surfaces. It is made up of steps and tools much the same as recipes for cooking a gourmet meal or following a pattern to sew an article of clothing. It traditionally employs the use of patterns, so drawing skills are not necessary.

Decorative painting, no matter what style or look, is made up of brushstrokes that enable the painter to control his or her brush to create detailed and elaborate designs. The fundaments of decorative painting lie in the understanding and mastering of brush control and brushstrokes.

Decorative painting is suitable for just about any surface, including furniture, accessories, walls, floors, ceilings, doors and more. Decorative painters have a saying: "If it doesn't move, I'll paint on it!" Decorative painting can be successfully combined with most of the painted finishes in this book.

Decorative painting uses all types of painting mediums, including oils, alkyds, acrylics and watercolors. No matter what painting medium you use, the basic principles are the same.

There are six primary brushstrokes in decorative painting: pull stroke, comma or polliwog stroke, line stroke, "S" stroke, "C" stroke and "U" stroke. There are four brush loading/blending strokes to learn: double-

KEYS TO SUCCESS
❧ When combining decorative painting with other painted finishes, it is important to coordinate color. Keep in mind also that too many intense, elaborate patterns on one surface or room will tend to fight each other when given the opportunity.
❧ Practice and repetition is essential to learning the basic strokes of decorative painting. Just as you learned to write the ABCs, so must you practice these strokes.
❧ For painting in oils, alkyds and watercolors, red sable brushes are recommended. For painting in acrylics, synthetic brushes are suitable.
❧ You may practice these techniques in any painting medium; just thin paints with the corresponding medium as noted. Use turpentine for oils and alkyds; use water for acrylics and watercolors.

Materials needed:
Oil, alkyd, acrylic or watercolor paints
Numbers 1 and 3 round brushes; numbers 4, 8 and 10 flat brushes; liner brush
Corresponding thinner
Palette and palette knife
Paper towels
Cotton rags

loading a brush, side-loading a brush, dry-brush blending and pat blending. Once you practice and learn the six primary brushstrokes and four brush loading/blending strokes, you'll be able to handle almost any subject in decorative painting.

PREPARATION
To practice the six primary brushstrokes, use a flat, round or liner brush.

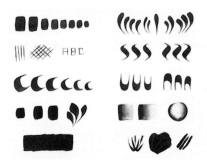

The basic brushstrokes and brush loading/blending strokes are the foundation to decorative painting. Master them, and you'll master decorative painting.

Thin paint to a thin, flowing consistency with its corresponding medium. In the examples shown here, red sable flat and round brushes and oils were selected.

To create double-loading, side-loading, dry-brush blending and pat blending, thin paints only slightly to a thick, creamy consistency with their corresponding medium. A flat brush was employed in all four techniques.

PULL STROKE
The pull stroke is the most basic of all brushstrokes in decorative painting. You simply load the brush with paint, touch the surface, apply pressure to the brush, drag it, and immediately lift up.

COMMA OR POLLIWOG STROKE

The most recognizable brushstroke is the comma or polliwog stroke. It is the most important brushstroke to master, for it develops total brush control. Load the brush with paint. Holding the brush at an angle, touch it to the surface and apply pressure to form the head of the stroke. As you begin to release pressure on the brush, curve the brush to the right or left, bringing it up to form a tail to the stroke. When using a round brush, twirl the brush slightly as you lift it up, forming a point with the bristles, which will form the tail of the stroke. When using the flat brush, angle the brush upward, making a chisel edge to form the stroke's tail.

LINE STROKE

The line stroke is, as the name implies, a singular, linear stroke. Use the chisel edge of a flat brush or the point of the round brush to make the line stroke. Touch the brush to the surface. Drag the brush across the surface at a consistent pressure to create a line that has the same thickness throughout. Apply less pressure for finer lines, heavier pressure for thick lines.

"S" STROKE

The "S" stroke forms a shape similar to an "S." Load the brush with paint. Holding it at an angle, draw a line stroke. Curve the brush to the right; apply pressure, dragging the brush to form a pull stroke. Begin to lift up on the pressure, curving to the left to form another line stroke at an angle. A backwards "S" stroke can also be completed by reversing the direction of the strokes just described.

"C" Stroke

The "C" stroke is similar to the "S" stroke. Load the brush with paint. Touch the brush's tip to the surface; drag the brush to make a short line stroke. Apply pressure to the brush while, at the same time, curving the brush to the right. As you reach the bottom of the curve, begin releasing pressure to come back to the brush's point or chisel edge, and drag the brush for another short line stroke.

"U" Stroke

To form the "U" stroke, load the brush with paint. Stand the brush on its tip and drag it downward to form a line. As you reach the bottom, apply pressure to the brush while curving the brush upward. Pull the brush back up to form a line stroke going upward.

Double-Loading

To double-load a brush means to carry two colors on the brush side by side, with a smooth blend in between. It's easier to double-load a flat brush. Make two piles of paint mixed with medium to a thick, creamy consistency. Flatten the piles with a palette knife to form a clean, low edge to stroke up against. Begin loading one half of the brush with the lighter color. Stroke *both* sides of that half of the brush through the paint. Now, stroke the other half of the brush along the darker color. Move the brush to a new area on the palette. Make short pull strokes to blend the two colors together in the center of the brush. Restroke along each pile of paint and blend until the brush is saturated.

SIDE-LOADING

To side-load a brush means to carry one color on one half of the brush. The paint is loaded in such a manner that it softly blends away on one side with a crisp color line definition on the other. Begin by dipping the brush into the painting medium, blotting on a paper towel, and stroking one half of the brush along the paint pile. Move the brush to a new area on the palette and stroke in short pull strokes, blending the color into the medium until there's no discernible definition of where the color stops and the medium begins.

DRY-BRUSH BLENDING

Dry-brush blending is critical to decorative painting with a shaded three-dimensional look. In this technique, you blend the colors on the surface very lightly in order not to remove the level of contrast between colors or remove too much paint. Begin by applying two colors side by side on the surface. Then wipe the brush on a rag or paper towel— *don't* clean the brush in medium. Now, stroke from one color into the other to soften the distinct division line between colors. The brush should just gently dust the surface. Wipe the brush often on a rag or paper towel. Continue until you have a smooth transition between colors, with very few brushstrokes visible.

PAT BLENDING

Pat blending softens one color into another like dry-brush blending, but visible brushmarks are left on purpose. Pat blending is used for creating effects such as vein sections on leaves and ripples in flower petals. Place two colors side by side and do some quick dry-brush blending. Now, start at the darkest or lightest point and stroke a series of pull strokes, one overlapping another to form streaks. The streaks can stay consistent in width or change from small to large or large to small. They can also stay straight or curve to create a rippling effect. Continue pat blending from one color into another until you achieve a smooth transition.

FLOWERS AND LEAVES DECORATIVE DESIGN

Florals can be painted in many different color schemes—from soft, romantic pastels to vibrant, rich hues. If there is already a floral design in the room on wallpaper, fabric, artwork or an accessory, this can be a starting point for determining colors as well as painting style.

Floral designs are best suited for powder rooms, bedrooms, elegant foyers and sitting rooms. Complementing techniques that work well with floral decorative painting include marbleizing, gilding and antiquing. Floral design work can be applied to furniture, accessories or on walls. For easier application of floral design to a wall, you can paint on a wallpaper border and then apply the paper to the wall.

PREPARATION

Thoroughly seal the surface. (See pages 10-19.) Base coat with the desired color and apply several light mistings of clear acrylic spray. Trace the floral design on page 85 on a sheet of tracing paper and transfer it to the surface with graphite paper. To transfer, position the traced design on the surface and tape it in place. Slip gray graphite paper (for light-colored surfaces) or white transfer paper (for dark surfaces) under the tracing. Lightly go over the design with a pen. Place the colors you need on the palette and whip them with the palette knife. Create a mix of titanium white plus burnt alizarin. Develop a light pink mixture and add a good deal of turpentine to get a thin, creamy consistency.

A decorative design of a mixed bouquet of roses, daisies, blossoms and leaves lends itself to many surfaces including furniture, accessories and even walls.

KEYS TO SUCCESS

❧ For effective decorative painting, you should have a good handle on the basic brushstrokes and brush blending techniques. (See pages 72-75.)

❧ Do not apply too much paint to the surface when blocking in colors, or you'll have trouble in the blending process. Apply just enough paint to reach an opaque coverage.

❧ Block in color, then complete an initial blending to break up the division lines between colors. Make choppy crisscross strokes using a flat brush.

❧ Use an extremely light touch on a flat or mop brush for the final blending—when you soften brushstrokes and color variations. This will create a minimum of visible brushstrokes and prevent you from overblending.

❧ Don't lose contrast within an object by overworking it. Once you achieve an initial smooth blend, stop and move on.

❧ These photographs show the whole painting being developed so you can see how each object looks at various stages. In reality, it will be easier for you to paint objects one at a time, from background to foreground, from start to finish.

Materials needed:
Tracing paper
Pen
Graphite paper/white transfer paper
Artists' oil paints in titanium white, burnt umber, leaf green dark, leaf green light, Payne's gray, burnt alizarin, burnt sienna, cadmium yellow, medium and ice blue
Base coat bristle brush or sponge brush; red sable brush; numbers 8, 10 and 12 flat brushes; number 3 round brush; and number 1 liner brush
Palette and palette knife
Towels
Painting medium (for thinning paint to flowing consistency for fine-line work and curlicues)
Turpentine
Clear acrylic spray

STEP 1. Double-load a number 8 flat brush with burnt umber and leaf green dark. Stroke three times for each leaf: at the leaf's base, along the left side, and along where the vein will be. Base the daisy petals in a brushstroke of white plus Payne's gray. Double-load a number 10 flat brush with white and burnt alizarin and stroke at the base of each blossom petal.

STEP 2. Double-load a flat brush with leaf green light and ice blue, and stroke at the right side and along the vein area of the leaves. Block in remaining areas of leaves with leaf green light. Overstroke daisy petals with flat or round brushes with thin consistency white. Block in remaining areas of blossom petal with white. Double-load a number 12 flat brush with the light pink mix and burnt alizarin. Stroke on the bowl of the rose with a combination of "U" strokes.

STEP 3. Blend leaves with a flat brush, using the dry-brush blending method. Base daisy and blossom centers with a "C" stroke of a double-loaded number 8 flat brush with burnt sienna and cadmium yellow medium. Fill in the remaining centers with yellow. Continue to stroke in individual petals on the rose with a double-loaded flat brush of pink and burnt alizarin. The side petals are made up of comma strokes.

STEP 4. To create leaf vein sections, pat blend angled streaks of white and ice blue from the center vein. Pat blend white on the daisy and blossom centers using a number 8 flat brush. Add pollen dots of burnt umber, burnt sienna and white around the centers. Continue adding brushstrokes with the double-loaded brush onto the rose. Add small filler petals where they are needed. Complete with scroll work with thinned green using the liner brush.

FRUITS AND LEAVES DECORATIVE DESIGN

A combination of fruits and leaves (or fruits and vegetables) is a popular design theme for furniture and accessories in kitchens, breakfast rooms, great rooms, and country-style rooms. Fruits and vegetables can be used together or independently, and tend to suggest a harvest theme, so a painted basket or bowl would be a natural accent in your designs. Kitchen cabinetry and furniture surfaces are ideal for this type of decorative painting. Due to their vibrant colors, choose fruit themes when you desire a lot of rich color in a given area. Complementing techniques that work well with fruits and leaves, or fruit and vegetable decorative painting include woodgraining, antiquing and glazing.

PREPARATION

Seal the surface to be painted thoroughly (see pages 10-19). Base coat with the desired color and apply several light mistings of clear acrylic spray. Trace the fruit design on page 84 on a sheet of tracing paper. Place the colors you'll need onto the palette and use a palette knife to whip them with a few drops of turpentine. Transfer the pattern to the surface with graphite paper (see page 76).

A harvest of fruits makes an ideal design element to be painted in kitchens and breakfast rooms.

KEYS TO SUCCESS

❧ When mixing fruits and vegetables in the same design, you must balance the colors to create harmony in the design. It is equally important to establish a balance of weight. Do not cause an imbalance by placing all the larger elements to one side.

❧ Follow the lines of the design carefully; if you allow objects to grow too much from their original shape, they will look out of proportion. Cut back color if you expand beyond design lines.

❧ On dark background surfaces, base coat the entire design area in several coats of acrylic white.

❧ Block in colors first, and complete an initial blending to break up the division lines between colors. Make choppy crisscross strokes using a flat brush.

❧ If you lose contrast during the blending process, add more dark and light tones and lightly blend them into the base color.

❧ Use an extremely light touch on a flat or mop brush during the final blending process—when you soften brushstrokes and color variations.

❧ These photographs show the whole painting being developed so you can see how each object looks at various stages. In reality, it will be easier for you to paint objects one at a time, from background to foreground, from start to finish.

Materials needed:
Artists' oil color paints in titanium white, cadmium red light, cadmium red medium, cadmium yellow medium, burnt sienna, burnt umber, cadmium orange, yellow ochre, Prussian blue, leaf green dark, ice blue, permanent green light and mauve; acrylic or latex paint for base coat
Sponge brush for base coat; red sable numbers 2, 8, 10 and 12 flat brushes; red sable number 3 round brush; and number 1 liner brush
Palette and palette knife
Paper towels
Turpentine
Clear acrylic spray
White acrylic base coat (if you're working on a dark surface)
Tracing paper
Graphite paper and a pencil

STEP 1. Begin basing the fruit and leaves in either oil or acrylic colors with a flat brush the size that is appropriate for the size of the object. Base leaves in leaf green dark, apple in cadmium red medium, pear and peach in cadmium yellow medium, and grapes in Prussian blue.

STEP 2. Establish the dark tones of each object. Apply dark-value green to the base of each leaf and blend. Overstroke leaf edges with white, pulling strokes in toward the center. Place red plus burnt sienna at the base of the apple and at its stem. Shade the right side of the pear with burnt sienna. Shade the peach by placing alizarin crimson at the bottom and in the crevice, then pick up cadmium yellow and blend it into the alizarin areas. Establish mid-value grapes with a mixture of deep blue plus white.

STEP 3. Add white highlights to each object by placing a touch of white on the subject and lightly blending it into the base tones. Define any objects that have "grown" during painting and blending; stroke them back to their natural shapes with a liner brush. Establish stems of leaves and fruits with a brown/black mixture. Outline one side of the lighter-value grapes with a thin stroke of light blue.

STEP 4. Continue to define each object with the liner brush: Add yellow markings to the apple, brown dot marks to the pear, additional alizarin crimson to the peach, and highlights to stems. Finish the grapes with simple, bright white dots. Strengthen all fruit highlights with additional white. Add curlicues of light green with a liner brush and thin consistency paint.

Designing with Fabrics and Wallpaper

A natural aspect of creating painted finishes and decorative design work is coordinating with fabric and wallpaper patterns. Your task is to make multiple patterns work together. Combining patterns and designs that do not coordinate well can cause a "pattern fight." In this situation, the viewer's eye will not travel smoothly from one surface to another but rather jump back and forth, becoming tired and confused. The best way to avoid this is to plan out every major aspect of the interior space, including furniture, walls, floors, ceilings, and window treatments.

Choose one item you feel is a focal point of the room—let this be your starting point. It could be a fabric or wallpaper print. If you use multiple patterns—for example, a floral chintz fabric with a stripe fabric, flowing bow fabric, and textured woven fabric—you would pick the floral chintz as the dominant pattern. You would then extract the center of the focus of this pattern to create your own design. The way in which the design will be used (on interior surface or furniture/accessory surface) will determine how you should plan your new design. The three most popular design choices would be a linear design, centralized design or a continuous free-form design (see pages 82-83). The linear design is best applied to interior surfaces, the centralized design works best on furniture and accessories, while the free-form design can work on furniture or interior surfaces.

Keys to Success

❧ When you design with the combination of fabric or wallpaper prints and painted finishes/decorative design, thorough planning of the entire room is crucial.

❧ Multiple patterns/designs in a room will tend to fight with one another unless you choose one dominant and other coordinated subordinate patterns.

❧ Let the pattern of the fabric or wallpaper be your guide to designing your painted work. Pick out key elements in the manufactured pattern and use them in your painted design.

It is not necessary to include every element of the fabric or wallpaper pattern in the new design.

❧ When you're not sure what to include, always simplify rather than elaborate on a design. Most times the simplest look is far more effective than one filled with too many elements.

Materials needed:
Tracing paper pad, 12 by 16 inches
Pencils in various leads, from 4H to 2B
Fine-line black marker
Large white artists' eraser
Acetate pad, 12 by 16 inches, .003 thickness
24-inch ruler
Scissors
Repositionable tape

RASPBERRY AND BLACKBERRY DESIGN

The overall pattern of raspberries and blackberries on fabric was the basis of a linear pattern: Individual berries were drawn onto a curving, continuous, linear vine. Leaves were added between the berry clusters. Free-flowing curlicues coming off the vine aid in creating a looseness to the design. This design can be adapted for furniture as well as built-in interior surfaces such as cabinets and display shelves.

VIOLET DESIGN

A cluster of violets and leaves were adapted from a fabric pattern into a linear design that was applied as a wall border. The violets are drawn coming off a curving vine with violet leaves and ivy leaves to add to the graceful line. The curlicues enhance the flow and looseness of the design.

ROSE DESIGN

A baroque-style fabric pattern of roses creates a foundation for the centralized design that was adapted from it. A base of flowers develops a free-form flow in two directions.

LINEAR DESIGN

STEP 1. Begin with the center of focus and build a curvy, linear flow. The design should be able to bend in many directions to wrap around furniture or interior shapes.

STEP 2. Draw subordinate elements off the main subject following the general design flow. Place these elements on the top and/or bottom of the main design. Detail strokes or curlicues can loosen up the design.

CENTRALIZED DESIGN

STEP 1. The centralized design will tend to have a circular or oblong shape. Begin with the center of focus.

STEP 2. Build subordinate elements off the main area on all sides, top and bottom. These elements should work off the center of focus and should not be placed separately.

Free-Form Design

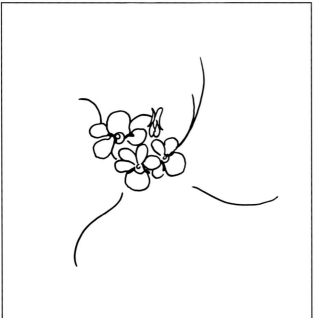

STEP 1. Once again, begin with the center of focus to build the design. A free-form design should not have a lot of weight to the design in any given area. Minimize the center of focus.

STEP 2. Build off the center of focus in several directions, allowing subordinate elements to flow independently. These elements should relate to the whole design but can have some separate qualities of their own.

Adapting a Design

STEP 1. Simplify the pattern of the fabric or wallpaper when creating your own design. Determine the center of focus by choosing large, colorful or interesting items. Don't attempt to include every element from the original source in the new design. Cross out elements that are not necessary—eliminate them in your mind or literally mark them off with a black marker on a sheet of acetate.

STEP 2. Trace the major elements off the pattern using a fine-line marker and a sheet of acetate. Loosely draw or trace the shapes—it's not necessary to trace exactly. Remember, you are *adapting* from this pattern; you are not out to copy it exactly.

STEP 3. Now make a clean pattern. You'll restructure the original design into a linear design, centralized design, or free-form design. Start with the center of focus and build off that area with subordinate elements from the original design.

These patterns are provided for you to use as guidelines for your decorative painting. They also can be simplified into stencils for use on any surface, or they can simply provide ideas for you to adapt your own design from. If you wish to use a design as is, simply trace the design from the book with tracing paper and a fine-line black marker. Center the traced design onto your surface and tape it in place. Slip a sheet of gray graphite paper or white transfer paper underneath, and trace lightly over the lines of the design to transfer it to your surface. Don't trace the shaded areas; those will be filled in with paint (see pages 76-79). Now you're ready to paint.

(Above.) Fruit design in the style of Peter Ompir's work. This design is shown on pages 78-79. Place this design on small accessories or furniture for the kitchen.

(Right.) Classic floral design featuring roses, blossoms and a daisy. See pages 76-77 for painting directions. Place this design on a tray, bandbox or other accessory.

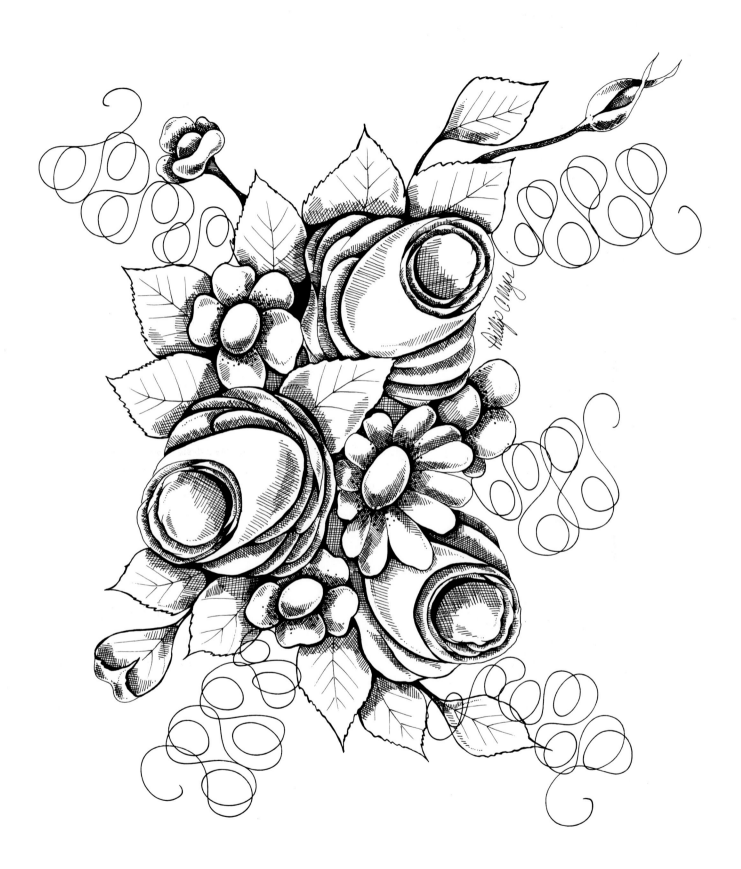

(Near right.) Baroque-style floral and scroll motif, great as an accent on slender spaces such as a narrow chair back panel. Gold leaf the background first, then paint the design on top for an elegant look.

(Right.) Blossoms and bow design ideal for placement on furniture drawer fronts. Paint the bow first, let it dry, then paint the leaves and blossoms.

(Far right.) Baroque-style scroll designs suitable for decorative accents on drawer fronts of dressers and bureaus. You can paint them on or gild them with gold or silver leaf.

(Above.) A central design of daisies and violets is perfect for the top of a small surface such as a step stool. Paint the design over a plastic wrap texturized background for added interest.

(Right.) A corner design of roses, daisies and a poppy is perfect for a tabletop. Paint the design in opposite corners to frame the table's surface.

(Right.) Place this panel of baroque-style scrolls and delicate rose vines on an edge of the top of a piece of furniture. Repeat, with variations as needed, to trim the furniture's edge.

(Above.) A circle of baroque-style scroll work would be ideal on the side of a piece of furniture. Paint or gild the scroll design.

(Below.) Country-style design in the style of Peter Hunt (see page 3). Place it on a small tin or wooden bucket. Cut a stencil of this design and paint a repeating pattern for a wall border.

(Left.) Repeat the larger version of this heart, tulip and brushstroke design along a kitchen table's edge for an eye-catching border. A smaller heart, tulip and brushstroke design can be used on a bread or cracker tray.

(Top.) A centralized version of this design is ideal for a tile backsplash in a kitchen or on a canister set.
(Bottom.) Use the largest version of this design and apply it to a wall or furniture surface. (See pages 40-41 for stenciling instructions.)

Chapter 9. Finishing Methods

You've completed your painted finish or decorative design work, and after many hours of careful attention to the paint application and blending on a furniture, accessory or interior surface you feel everything's finished. Well, not quite. After you've finished painting your surface, there's still one more very important step you must take: applying the protective finish. If left undone, your creative work can be damaged.

Varnish Application

As you will see, you can apply a varnish finish, a paste-wax finish, or a combination of the two. The finished effect you desire and the amount of protection the painted surface needs will determine which method to use. A varnish finish creates depth in your paint effects, while a paste-wax finish allows you to feel the paint qualities. A varnish finish provides a great deal of protection, especially when applied in a series of layered coats, while a paste-wax finish provides a minimum amount of protection. If you prefer the look of paste wax, you can apply varnish first and then paste wax on top of it.

Many different types of varnish finishes will work effectively for your needs. The surface on which you have painted (furniture, wall or floor) does not exclusively affect your varnish selection. You should consider the type of painting you've completed to determine which type of varnish to use. There are

Keys to Success

❧ A benefit in applying a varnish over your painted finish or decorative design work is the enhancement of painted colors. Many colors in oil, alkyd and acrylic mediums dry with a dull film over them. A coat of varnish will revive these hues and bring back their true appearance—as if they were wet.

❧ An object that will receive minimal handling (such as a decorative accessory piece) requires basic protection (one to three coats of varnish), while an object such as a table that will endure extensive use needs heavy protection (four to eight coats).

❧ Avoid using water-based varnish over excessively slick enamel painting, because the varnish will bead up on the surface.

❧ Seal gold and silver leaf with an oil- or resin-based varnish; water-based varnish can cause tarnishing of the leaf.

❧ For wood surfaces that have been coated with wood sealer, the varnishing step becomes easier. The wood sealer has already closed the wood's pores, preventing the varnish from soaking into the surface, thus requiring fewer coats.

❧ Both spray-on and brush-on varnishes can provide similar results. Just keep in mind that a spray-on varnish will require more applications to achieve a finished look that a brush-on can produce in fewer applications.

❧ You must allow for proper drying time of the painted surface before applying a varnish. For acrylics and latex paints, allow at least three hours; for alkyds and enamels, twenty-four hours; and for oils, anywhere from forty-eight hours to three weeks. Remember, the thicker the application of paint, the longer it will take to dry.

❧ The art of a good-looking varnish finish is in how you apply it to the surface. Be sure to work in a clean, dust- and lint-free environment.

❧ When varnishing with a brush-on product, do not stroke a given area too many times or brushstroke marks will form and dry into the finish. Coat an area with an even application, and move on.

❧ Do not attempt any dry sanding in the finishing process. Only wet sanding with fine sandpaper, soap and water should be used over coats of varnish.

Materials needed:
Oil-based, lacquer-based, polyurethane-based or water-based varnish
High-quality, natural-bristle varnish brushes and sponge brushes
Mineral spirits, lacquer thinner or water
Tack cloths
Wet/dry sandpapers, numbers 400 to 600
Soap bar

SPRAY-ON VARNISH

When spraying, light coats are preferred to heavy applications. Allow each coat to dry thoroughly before applying another; otherwise, you could accidentally "lift off" a previous coat.

STEP 2. If you desire a heavy-depth look to the varnish finish, you'll need to build up the varnish by applying a series of three coats, wet sanding the surface, then applying three more coats. To wet sand, sprinkle the dry varnish with water. Pick up a piece of wet/dry sandpaper and dip it in water, then rub the sandpaper across a bar of soap. Begin sanding in a small circular motion with very little pressure. Be careful! You can sand right down to the painting very quickly. The wet-sanding process will remove any imperfections in the varnish and prepare it for the next layer.

BRUSH-ON VARNISH

STEP 1. To apply a brush-on finish, you'll need a sponge brush or fine varnish brush. Stir the varnish (don't create too many bubbles when stirring), dip the brush into the varnish, and pull across the container's edge to remove excess. Begin at one end of the object and brush across to the other end. The varnish should flow on the surface. If your brush drags, it's too dry—you'll need more varnish on the brush.

STEP 3. After sanding, wipe away the surface with a tack cloth. The varnish will look hazy and scratched at this point, but that will disappear when you apply another coat of varnish or apply a paste-wax coating. Keep in mind that this is a very slow process, but the results will be worth the effort. The depth a varnish finish can add to your painted finish or decorative design is absolutely breathtaking.

oil-based, lacquer-based, polyurethane-based and water-based finishes on the market. An oil-based varnish is made from natural gums; it is ideal for finishing decorative design work or painted finishes completed in artists' oil and alkyd color on furniture and interiors. A lacquer finish is made from synthetic coatings and is ideal when you want a glossy finish over oils and alkyds on furniture and interiors. Polyurethane finishes are synthetic thermoplastic resins used when a tough, chemical- and wear-resistance is needed. Polyurethane finishes can be applied over oils, alkyds and acrylics and are ideal for protecting stenciling or painted finishes on floors. Water-based varnishes are made from acrylic polymers and are designed to protect acrylic painted finishes (although they also can be applied over thin oil and alkyd paintings). Water-based varnishes are one of the few finishes that are completely nonyellowing.

If you have completed your work in oils, enamels or alkyds, use an oil-based varnish; if the work was completed in latex or acrylics, use a water-based varnish. Keep in mind that you can apply a water-based varnish over oils and can apply an oil-based varnish over acrylics. An exception is when you've completed an oil painting with an extremely thick application of color. The oil medium, even after dry to the touch, requires a "breathing" space to prevent it from cracking and crazing over the years. An acrylic water-based varnish will not allow for any breathing to occur, thus possibly causing problems down the road.

PASTE-WAX APPLICATION

You can create a finish with a rich, hand-rubbed quality with a few simple steps. There are three distinct approaches you can take when applying a paste-wax finish over decorative design

work on furniture and accessories: varnish plus paste wax, antique paste wax, and direct paste wax. Each one provides a slightly different finished effect. Experiment on sample pieces to determine your preference.

Once your painted finish in oils, alkyds, enamels, acrylics or latex has thoroughly cured, you are ready to apply the paste-wax method of your choice. A paste-wax finish should only be completed on items that will not receive a tremendous amount of heavy-duty use. The finish will provide a protective coating, but will not create a coating that can withstand heavy abuse like a varnish finish could.

If you desire a hand-rubbed finish over the painted surface without the depth and sheen of varnish, try a direct application of paste wax (without any varnish). Keep in mind, when applying a direct paste-wax finish over the painted surface, there will be some softening

---

KEYS TO SUCCESS

❧ A heavy application of paste wax does not mean you'll receive better protection for your painted surface. You can cut through the build-up of wax in seconds. By comparison, every layer of varnish you place on the surface will protect a piece substantially.

❧ For surfaces that require a good deal of protection, such as items that will be handled and used a lot, consider a varnish coating and then a paste-wax finish.

❧ To create the color-tinted, antique paste-wax finish, you will actually mix oil colors into the paste wax before

applying it to the surface. This will create an old-world look to the finish.

❧ Your paste-wax finish applied to the painted surface will be fairly durable. It will only need dusting and cleaning with a dry, cotton rag. Then, once a year, lightly recoat the surface with a fresh coat of paste wax and buff to a luster.

Materials needed:
Paste wax, containing carnauba wax
Cheesecloth
Cotton cloths
Tack cloth
Varnish and varnish brush
Artists' oil paints in burnt umber, asphaltum
Palette and palette knife

VARNISH AND PASTE-WAX FINISH

For this type of finish, apply coats of varnish as explained on pages 94-95. Let them dry, and then apply paste wax. You can apply a good deal of pressure when buffing, due to the layers of varnish protecting the painted surface.

of the colors, creating an aged look to the surface. Also, when applying this direct finish over a painted surface, you may wear off parts of the painting. This can occur during the buffing process when heavy pressure is applied to the surface. This warning may scare the faint at heart, but if you especially desire an old-world, worn effect, this accident can be to your benefit. It achieves a "worn by the test of time" look—without the wait of natural aging.

ANTIQUE PASTE WAX

STEP 1. For an aged, antique paste-wax finish, spoon out several teaspoons of paste wax onto the palette. Pick up some burnt umber and asphaltum on the tip of a palette knife, and mix them thoroughly into the paste wax. Coat the surface with the paste-wax/oil color mixture using a cloth. Let it dry five to ten minutes.

STEP 2. Buff the surface to a luster using a cotton cloth and a circular motion. The wax mixture will age and mellow all bright hues on your painted surface, creating a beautiful, old-world look.

DIRECT PASTE WAX

STEP 1. First, make sure the surface is free of dirt. To remove any particles, lightly wipe the surface with a tack cloth. Now, using a cotton cloth, lightly apply a thin, even coat of paste wax. When working on wood, stroke with the direction of the grain.

STEP 2. Allow the wax to dry to a haze (five to ten minutes), then buff with a piece of cheesecloth or cotton cloth. Use some pressure when buffing, but remember that there is no coating between your painted work and the wax. If you don't want the "worn look," be careful—you could easily rub away fine details in the painted surface.

Floral Bedroom

This well-designed bedroom features a deep pink strié finish on the walls with a stenciled wall border, sheets with hand-painted tulips, a stenciled lampshade, and two decorative painted shadow boxes with florals. The bandboxes on the bed have a light green combed finish. The combed finish is completed by making marks into a wet glaze with a combing tool, similar to the initial steps of creating the moiré finish.

A Country-Style Kitchen

(Left.) Simple, country-style, hand-painted tiles along with a sponge-painted tabletop create a colorful, crisp look. The ladder-back chairs have a light blue strié and flyspecking finish with hand-painted hearts, tulips and leaves.

Raspberries and Blackberries in a Kitchen

A combination raspberry and blackberry design accents a few kitchen cabinet doors in this kitchen. The design work was adapted from fabric used in drapes and seat cushions in the room.

Decorated Table

The sponged walls create a dramatic background for the decorative painting on the table and display case. The round breakfast table received a black base coat that was distressed to show the wood beneath. A raspberry and blackberry design was then painted on a cream-colored border around the perimeter of the table. Small groupings of berries were painted on the table's base.

Painted Display Case

The raspberry and blackberry trim around the top and sides of this display case ties in with other elements in the kitchen. The walls received opaque sponging in several shades of medium to light pink, plus a cream tone.

VIOLET BEDROOM

A feminine bedroom features a border
of hand-painted violets and leaves
around the perimeter. The violet design
was adapted from the fabric used for the
drapes, pillows and comforter.

MASCULINE DEN

A rich, dramatic color scheme decorates
this den. A painted mahogany woodgrain has been applied to crown molding, doors, and judge's paneling
throughout the entire room.

DETAIL OF MAHOGANY WOODGRAIN

To create this mahogany woodgrain, base coat the surface with a very deep red-brown, flat latex paint. (Create a brown similar to 50 percent burnt umber plus 50 percent black, using flat latex paint instead of artists' colors.) Then, create a glaze by adding a mixture of 60 percent water and 40 percent acrylic varnish to the brown paint. Working on a small section at a time (one panel, for example), brush on the glaze with a base coat bristle brush. Quickly, while it remains wet, work in the glaze with the flogger brush. First, pat the surface with the flat end of the brush in short, hopping motions. Then, lightly drag the brush over these marks (similar to the strié technique). The pat-hop brush marks create dots and dashes, and the strié brush marks create linear grain markings. Several applications of an oil-based polyurethane varnish bring out the subtle color variations in the markings.

DETAIL OF PAINTED CEILING
Here you can see the intricacies of the painted finishes this ceiling received.

PAINTED CEILING
The painted ceiling displays sponge-painted molding, stripes of gold paint, a beige fantasy-style marbleizing, and gilded gold panels.

GARDEN SCENE

This trompe l'oeil wall showcases a
painted wisteria tree with flowers and a
sponged stone wall with arches that
look out on a scenic pastoral landscape.
The floor is a painted garden of slate,
white stones and grass.

PAINTED CASTLE DOORS

Is it real? Trompe l'oeil castle doors feature
deep, rich brown woodgrain painted directly on the wall surface. The floor is a
trompe l'oeil garden, with painted slate,
white stones and grass.

PEACH DINING ROOM

The walls of this dining room are peach-colored with plastic wrap texturizing. To add further decorative elements, a bow, ribbon and leaf design has been painted at the top edge and peach fantasy marble panels have been added below.

DETAIL OF DINING ROOM

Plastic wrap texturizing combines beautifully with the decorative painting on top of it, creating an attractive wall border in this dining room.

SPONGE-PAINTED LAUNDRY ROOM

(Above.) The walls in this laundry room feature blue and white sponge work. A complementing manufactured wallpaper border was chosen for the top edge.

TEXTURIZED BATHROOM WALLS

(Left.)The blue bathroom walls exhibit plastic wrap texturizing for an exciting, active pattern that replaces wallpaper, typically used in bathrooms.

FOYER WITH WOODGRAINING

A fantasy woodgrain effect was applied
to the walls, panel sections, and all the
molding in this foyer. Dramatic mirrors
magnify the painted finish.

DETAIL OF WOODGRAINING

Here you can see the rich coloration of the fantasy woodgrain,
painted on foyer walls and molding.

CONTEMPORARY CONDO

A bright, vivid palette was chosen to decorate this open-style condominium. The chair rail molding was masked and painted several colors, thus creating striking color bands. The checkerboard squares on the kitchen walls were hand-painted. In the background is a blue canvas tarp, painted with the glazing and sponging techniques, and stretched over a metal frame to create an inexpensive room divider.

DETAIL OF CONDO

A kitchen sponge was used to paint the walls of the sitting area. Two shades of green and two shades of pink were applied with a rectangular sponge to leave definite shapes.

PAINTED FLOOR

(Left.) In this foyer, a graphic tile pattern was painted for a bold statement in black, white and gray. A white base coat was applied, then gray tile shapes added, then black diamond shapes were stenciled. The walls have a transparent gray sponged finish. (The tabletop is real marble!)

CLASSIC LIVING ROOM

(Right.) The walls feature ragging above, woodgraining below, gold leaf chair rail and inset panels. The tabletop features green serpentine marbleizing with candle followers that have gold leaf shades. The drawer handle, molding and leg tips were also gilded.

PAINTED PIE SAFE AND CHAIR

The pie safe, bread box, and chair feature light purple strié and flyspecking finishes. Cornflowers and pink ribbons were painted on the furniture to coordinate with the wallpaper's design.

PAINTED CHEST OF DRAWERS

A hand-painted design of bow, ribbon, blossoms and leaves ties in two wallpaper patterns: the bow coordinates with the bedroom's wallpaper border, while the blossoms and leaves tie in the bathroom's wallpaper. Ruling pink lines trim out each drawer front.

SPONGE-PAINTED KITCHEN

(Left.) The walls of this kitchen display a soft, pink transparent sponging with a stenciled border along the top and bottom edges of the wall.

VICTORIAN LIVING ROOM

Transparent sponging has been applied to the walls along with a complementing stenciled design at the chair rail and crown molding areas. The mantel features black marbleizing along with white alabaster marbleizing.

ELEGANT FOYER

(Right.) The walls of this foyer received a pink moiré painted finish to coordinate with the fabric of the table skirt. A decorative bird design has been painted over the doorway to tie in with a wallpaper pattern of birds in the hallway.

GRAPE SCREEN

The background of this decorative wall screen was developed to imitate a thickly textured leather panel. Heavy vellum tracing paper was crumpled and stuck to the surface with acrylic varnish, then stained with a burnt umber oil glaze. Clusters of grapes were hand-painted on top, along with bordering comma strokes and gold leaf baroque shapes.

Painted Wardrobe

The wardrobe's inner panels feature red plastic wrap texturizing applied to a black background. The panels were then masked out to create bands of gold for an extra decorative touch.

Art Deco Armoire

This Art Deco-style armoire displays masking and ruling techniques. A deep blue creates color bands around the doors and drawers, with fine-line work of gray and turquoise completed with the ruling technique. The tan areas are where the natural wood shows through.

Faux Marble Accent Piece

The corbel decorative accent piece of
two cherub faces was painted with a faux
brecciated marble finish. After the
painting was thoroughly dried a spray-
on varnish was applied due to ease of
application.

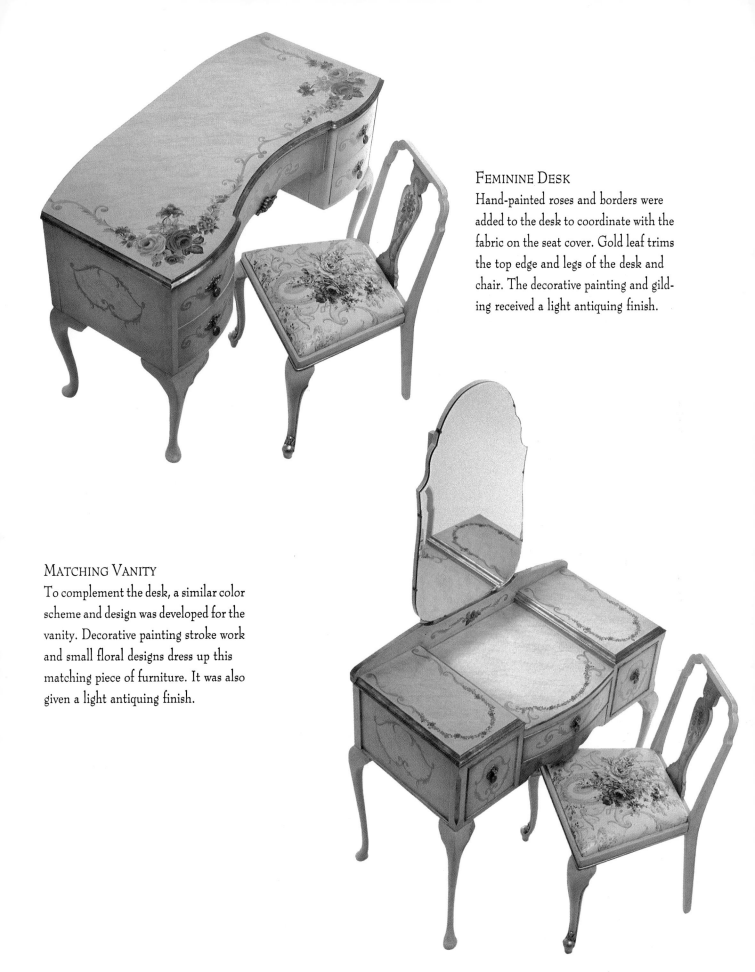

Feminine Desk

Hand-painted roses and borders were added to the desk to coordinate with the fabric on the seat cover. Gold leaf trims the top edge and legs of the desk and chair. The decorative painting and gilding received a light antiquing finish.

Matching Vanity

To complement the desk, a similar color scheme and design was developed for the vanity. Decorative painting stroke work and small floral designs dress up this matching piece of furniture. It was also given a light antiquing finish.

DINING ROOM CHAIR

An elegant dining room chair was created by duplicating the pattern of the seat cushion fabric on the back rest. Gold leaf was applied as a base, then a green, red and blue strié finish was added. Finally, the negative areas of the design were painted in black, allowing the gold and strié to show through.

ROSES ON SIDE TABLE

Roses were painted on the top of this side table. A cream-colored circle was the foundation, which received a transparent sponged background before the decorative painting.

COUNTRY-STYLE JELLY CABINET

A decorative country scene was painted on this double-door jelly cabinet, which then received a mid-level antiquing finish. The scenic design wraps around all three visible sides for a bold statement.

BAROQUE-STYLE BUREAU
This hand-painted bureau features
roses, daisies and leaves intermingled
with baroque-style borders and covered
with a light antiquing finish. Silver leaf
dresses up the edges, and the top was
painted with the green serpentine marbleizing technique.

HALL TREE
Decorative painted fruits and stroke work embellish this hall tree. Ruling lines trim the edges, while a medium antiquing finish in black ties the entire piece together.

PENNSYLVANIA DUTCH CABINET
This cabinet is painted with Pennsylvania Dutch-style folk art decorating all three sides. A whimsical farm couple adorn the front panel, while traditional hearts and strokes trim out the other sides of the cabinet. The whole cabinet received a light antiquing finish.

FIRE SCREEN BASKET

A cut-out fire screen in the shape of a basket is covered with hand-painted roses, leaves and a flowing bow. The basket even features individual basket weaves.

FLORAL DRESSER

A sponge-painted background of cream tones creates a neutral backdrop to paint a floral motif on the dresser top and drawer fronts. The ruling technique defines the edges in gold paint.

ROSES ON ARMOIRE
Hand-painted roses adorn the inset panels of this armoire. A transparent sponged background was first created, then the roses were added, and finally an earth-tone antiquing ages the piece.

KITCHEN SET

(Left.) A kitchen set of table, chairs, kitchen cabinet and accessories are all painted in the style of Peter Hunt (see page 3). Bright, colorful designs in a whimsical "peasant style" create a casual look. A light antiquing technique completes the finish.

BLUE CHAIR

A light blue strié finish was applied to the chair, and then blue daisies, cornflowers and leaves were painted on top in a monochromatic style. Blue striping trims out the edges, and an overall blue flyspeck finish completes the chair. (The background wall has a pink sponging finish, while the trim has strié. The floor is real wood.)

IVY STOOL

A stenciled ivy design was painted on the seat of the stool, then trimmed and defined with line work. The background wall was ragged with soft yellow tones.

PAINTED CHEST AND FLOOR

(Right.) A hand-painted chest features baroque-style design work with gold leaf accents and antiquing. The floor was painted with white alabaster marbleizing and black marbleizing techniques.

GLOSSARY

ABSTRACT — unrelated to reality in terms of painted finishes; the painted effect is not an imitation of natural objects.

ACRYLIC POLYMER — a thermoplastic resin, with a synthetic substance or mixture, used as a binder with powdered pigments in the creation of artists' acrylic colors.

ANTIQUING — the application of a very thin brown or black coating over a surface to make an object look older than it really is.

ARTISTS' ACRYLIC COLOR — paint that is a mixture of powdered pigments ground in thermoplastic, synthetic emulsions. It can be thinned and cleaned up with water.

ARTISTS' ALKYD COLOR — paint that is a mixture of powdered pigment ground in linseed oil. It must be thinned and cleaned up with mineral spirits or turpentine. Alkyds dry much faster than artists' oil colors.

ARTISTS' OIL COLOR — paint that is a mixture of powdered pigment ground in linseed oil. It must be thinned and cleaned up with mineral spirits or turpentine.

BADGER HAIR — an extremely soft hair taken from the face of a badger and used in the creation of artists' brushes.

BASE COAT — the initial application of paint to a surface.

BINDER — the agent that acts as a cohesive to join particles together; binders hold the powder pigments together in artists' colors.

BLOTCHY — a surface's irregular, disfiguring marks that are formed by accident; unwanted, noticeable patterns.

BURNISH — to polish, or to rub a surface with a hard tool, especially to adhere and smooth areas or remove loose areas of gold or silver leaf.

CAST COLOR — a reflection or shadow of one object's color on another object's surface.

CHOPPY BLENDING — a loose style of blending colors using a brush in short, quick strokes.

COLOR VALUES — the degrees of lightness, darkness, saturation and brightness of a hue.

CORBELS — decorative accents made of plaster, wood or stone; they project out from the face of a wall surface.

CORNICE — a horizontal architectural decorative strip molded or made from plaster, wood or stone; usually found just below the ceiling.

CRACKLED — when a surface shows random separations in its paint or varnish finish, making it appear older than it really is.

CRISSCROSS — a paint stroke that forms crossed lines, overlapping randomly, making "X" shapes.

CUT DOWN — to diminish the amount of color or varnish that is on the surface.

CUTTING COLOR — the reduction of paint on the surface.

DADO — the lower section of a wall (below the picture rail) decorated differently than the upper section.

DARK VALUE — the deeper color tones on the gray scale that can be created from any color by adding black.

DECORATIVE PAINTING — an ornamental art form used to decorate functional as well as nonfunctional surfaces; it is a teachable art form broken down in this book into step-by-step methods.

DISTRESS — to batter or beat a surface with the use of abrasive materials to create the illusion of long-term use and age.

DOUBLE-LOAD — to carry two colors on a brush at one time, side by side, with a smooth color gradation between them.

DRY-BRUSH BLENDING — to gradate and create a smooth color transition by stroking over a freshly painted surface with a brush loaded with very little dry paint; no thinning medium or solvent is present in the brush during this process.

EARTH TONES — colors that are made with natural pigments (like yellow ochre, which is made from refined clay).

ENAMEL — a paint made of a liquid mixture of powdered pigments plus resins, hydrocarbons, drier and additives. It must be thinned and cleaned up with mineral spirits or turpentine.

FANTASY FINISH — intended as a nonrealistic painted effect that may exaggerate the look of a real surface.

FAUX BOIS — the French term for fake or false woodgrain painted to represent any type of wood.

FLECKS — small particles of paint spattered on the surface.

FLYSPECKING — the painted finish technique that disperses small particles of paint over the surface with the use of a toothbrush and thin-consistency paint.

GESSO — a prepared paint made with plaster of Paris or gypsum, used as a primer and sealing coating to canvas, wood and plaster.

GILDING — the application of a layer of gold or silver leaf to a surface.

GLAZE — a transparent mixture of color plus painting medium.

GOLD LEAF — real or imitation gold that has been hammered into extremely delicate sheets five-millionths of an inch in thickness.

GRANITE — a hard, natural stone formation of quartz, feldspar and mica.

GRAY SCALE — a standardized chart of value changes from white to black (from lightest to darkest) in percentage increments.

GRID — a framed structure of equally spaced parallels and crossbars used to paint various tile patterns on floor surfaces. A grid is also used to enlarge or reduce the size of designs by scaling them up or down proportionately.

HAZE — a transparent but cloudy or smoky coating over a surface that obstructs the clarity of the color below.

HIGH CONTRAST — an extreme color value difference in close proximity; the highest level would be from white to gray to black in a short distance.

HUE — the quality of color; the intensity of a color, as in a shade or tint.

INK-LIKE CONSISTENCY — paint thinned with painting medium, painting glaze or solvent to the liquid state that matches drawing ink.

KNOCK BACK — the reduction of color or texture achieved by blending the paint on a surface.

KOLINSKY HAIR — hair from a particular squirrel bred in Russia for its fine red sable tail hairs. These hairs are used to make red sable brushes.

LACQUER THINNER — the solvent designed to thin and/or remove the synthetic-based finish of lacquer (a type of varnish).

LATEX — paint made from powdered pigment ground with emulsion of rubber or plastic globules. It can be cleaned up with water.

LIFT OFF — the intentional or accidental removal of base coat, paint finish or varnish.

LIGHT VALUE — the brighter color tones on the gray scale. Any color can become a light value by the addition of white.

MALACHITE — a green to nearly black mineral that is a basic carbonate of copper, with an intensive pattern of irregular, wavy half-arch shapes.

MARBLEIZING — the act of reproducing a marble pattern through the use of paint, applied with a brush and/or feathers on a surface.

MASKING — to mark off an area and then protect that area by covering with tape or other items so that it won't receive paint when a nearby area is being painted.

MEDIUM — the type of paint used, such as oils, acrylics or alkyds; or a liquid, such as varnish, linseed oil or turpentine, used to thin paints.

MEDIUM VALUE — a color tone that is, simply, not too dark and not too light; a shade in the middle from dark value to light value.

MELLOW HUE — a color that has a soft, aged appearance; color will emit qualities of yellow or gray.

MIDTONE — a center point of a color's value in relation to its lightest or darkest points within a given painted area.

MINERAL SPIRITS — a solvent strong enough to clean and thin oil-based paints, painting mediums and varnishes.

MODELED — to render or work a painted effect to represent a form or shape.

MOIRÉ — a wavy or watered pattern found in fabric weave; a painted-finish effect that mimics the fabric's pattern, applied with tools to a wet paint glaze.

MOTTLED — painted blotches of different colors on a surface.

MUDDY COLOR — a color that has been mixed with other colors to the point of losing its own clarity or brightness.

OPAQUE — paint coverage thick enough that light cannot pass through it.

OPEN TIME — the period in which the paints, painting mediums or varnishes will remain workable before they begin to set up and dry.

PAINT RUNS — usually undesirable drips of paint or varnish that move down a vertical surface.

PASTE WAX — a coating of specially designed wax for furniture that is rubbed on and adds a level of polish and sheen to a surface.

PAT BLENDING — the method by which paint colors are gradated through short pull strokes over a surface with a paint brush.

PATTERN — a guideline to follow when creating, as in woodworking, sewing or decorative painting.

PLASTER — a substance made of a mixture of lime, sand and water; it is molded and formed into various architectural or decorative shapes.

POROUS — a surface that has permeable openings which moisture easily penetrates.

PRIMER — an opaque, paint-like base coat application that seals the surface and readies it for decorative finishes.

RAGGING — a painted finish in which a mottled texture is created by patting a crumpled rag on a wet paint glaze.

RED SABLE — fine, natural animal hairs from a squirrel's tail used to create the highest quality artists' painting brushes.

RULING — the painted trim work of fine lines through the application of thin consistency paint with a ruling pen.

SET-UP TIME — the time it takes for the paint, painting medium or varnish to begin to dry and become tacky.

SIDE-LOAD — to carry color only on one side of the brush with painting medium or solvent on the other, creating a blended transition on the brush from opaque color to transparent color to no color.

SILVER LEAF — real or imitation silver that has been hammered into extremely delicate sheets of five-millionths of an inch in thickness.

SOLVENT — the agent that cleans and thins items such as paints, varnishes and painting mediums. A paint's solvent can be used as a painting medium.

SPACKLING COMPOUND — also called plaster patch, it is a thick-bodied, plaster-like substance that is used to fill holes in interior surfaces.

SPECTRUM — a total range of color; a band of colors into which a beam of light is dispersed by a prism.

SPONGING — the painted finish technique that uses the application of paint loaded on a sponge to create a textural pattern on the surface.

SPORADIC — an irregular and inconsistent pattern or timing.

SQUARE FOOTAGE — the total area of a surface calculated by multiplying the width by the length.

STENCIL — a sheet of Mylar, acetate or heavy card stock with a design cut into it.

STENCILING — the decorative application of design work achieved by brushing paint through a cut design opening (see *Stencil*).

STRIÉ — the painted finish technique that creates irregular linear streaks in a wet paint glaze through the use of a flogger brush.

STRIPPING—the removal of paint, varnish or other build-up on a surface through the use of commercially made chemical products and scraping tools.

TACKY—a sticky quality that develops during the drying time of a paint product. Some techniques require waiting for a tacky paint state before proceeding with the technique.

TEMPLATE—a manufactured pattern or mold to follow when creating, such as in woodworking, sewing or decorative painting.

TEXTURIZING—the painted finish technique that creates pattern something like alligator skin on a surface by pressing crumpled plastic wrap into a wet paint glaze.

THICK, CREAMY CONSISTENCY—a paint mixed with a very small amount of painting medium, paint glaze or solvent, whipped to the texture of whipped butter—paint should hold peaks when patted with palette knife.

THIN, CREAMY CONSISTENCY—a paint mixed with painting medium, paint glaze or solvent to the texture of whipped cream.

THIN, SOUPY CONSISTENCY—a paint mixed with painting medium, paint glaze or solvent to the texture of watered-down soup.

TOLE—the French term for tinware.

TOLE PAINTING—the decoration of tinware with designs of colorful brush-stroke work, begun in the sixteenth century in France.

TORTOISESHELL—the form that covers the body of a turtle; a pattern of earth-tone marks; a painted finish that duplicates its namesake.

TRANSPARENT—a coating of paint or glaze so thin that light can easily pass through; when something is transparent, you can see through it clearly.

TROMPE L'OEIL—the French term for fool the eye; a painting style that renders objects in life-size proportions, fooling the viewer into believing he or she is seeing real objects.

VALUE—the ratio or percentage of color that relates to the gray scale; a color from lightest to darkest.

VARNISH—a clear coating of either an oil-based, lacquer-based, polyurethane-based or water-based product that protects what is underneath the coating.

VEINS—the interior structural pattern element found in leaf structures as well as in marble surfaces.

VENEER—a thin wood panel applied to a surface with glue coating.

WASH—paint that is thinned with enough painting medium, painting glaze or solvent to make it transparent.

WET SANDING—the smoothing of a surface with a fine, wet/dry-style sandpaper, wet with water and soap. This application is completed in the finishing stage, removing any imperfections between coats of varnish.

WOODGRAIN—the pattern of marks found in wood surfaces; a flowing, organic pattern.

WOODGRAINING—the painted finish that duplicates a wood type through the use of a wet paint glaze, brushes and special woodgrain tools.

WOOD PORES—the openings found in between the grain markings that must be sealed for the wood to accept a painted finish.

WOOD PUTTY—the thick compound made of whiting, linseed oil, and binders in a dough-like consistency, used to fill imperfections on a wood surface before painting or finishing.

WOOD SEALER—a clear, varnish-like product that provides a coating that soaks in and closes the wood's pores, providing a paintable surface.

SOURCES

The following are sources around the country for supplies, materials and seminars.

A TOUCH OF CLASS BY AILEEN
9000 Caminito Drive NE
Albuquerque, NM 87111
(505)821-7224
Seminars, instruction books and supplies

ACCENT PRODUCTS
300 E. Main Street
Lake Zurich, IL 60047
(312)438-8207
Paints, graining and combing tools

ALLEN'S WOOD CRAFTS
3020 Dogwood Lane Route 3
Sapulpa, OK 74066
(918)224-8796
Wood accessories and small furniture pieces

AMES CUSTOM WOOD PRODUCTS
361 Engle Street
Escondido, CA 92029
(619)746-1950
Wood accessories and small furniture pieces

ARISTOCAST ORIGINALS
6200 Highlands Pkwy Suite 1
Smyrna, GA 30082
(404)333-9934
Cast molding, fireplace mantels, niches and ceiling medallions

BETTER WAY BRUSH PRODUCTS
P.O. Box 81619
Cleveland, OH 44181
(800)424-2787
Brush cleaning supplies

BINNEY & SMITH
P.O. Box 431
Easton, PA 18044
(215)250-5877
Artists' paints, brushes and supplies

ADELE BISHOP
P.O. Box 3349
Kinston, NC 28501
(919)527-4189
Stencil supplies

GRETCHEN CAGLE PUBLICATIONS
1711 Dogwood Court
Claremore, OK 74017
(918)341-5526
Seminars, instruction books and supplies

CARNIVAL ARTS, INC.
P.O. Box 4145
Northbrook, IL 60065
(708)949-4747
Spray paints and acrylic paints

CEDAR CREST
P.O. Box 387
Pleasanton, KS 66075
(913)352-6706
Seminars, instruction books and supplies

CHADSWORTH, INC.
P.O. Box 53268
Atlanta, GA 30355
(404)876-5410
Plaster and wood columns for interiors/exteriors

CHERRY TREE TOYS
P.O. Box 369
Belmont, OH 43718
(614)848-4363
Wood toys, clock parts, wheels and accessory pieces

CHROMA ACRYLICS
P.O. Box 510
Hainesport, NJ 08036
(609)261-3452
Artists' paints and mediums

COUNTRY STENCILS
1526 Marsetta Drive
Beavercreek, OH 45432
(513)426-5715
Stencils

DECO ART
P.O. Box 360
Stanford, KY 40484
(606)365-9739
Paints

DELTA/SHIVA
25550 Pellissier Place
Whittier, CA 90601
(213)686-0678
Artists' paints and supplies

DOWL-IT COUNTRY COTTAGE LINE
P.O. Box 310
Hastings, MI 49058
(616)945-5493
Wood furniture and accessories

GAIL GRISI STENCILING INC.
P.O. Box 1263
Haddonfield, NJ 08033
(609)354-1757
Stencils and supplies

M. GRUMBACHER INC.
30 Engelhard Drive
Cranbury, NJ 08512
(609)655-8282
Artists' paints and brushes

HOUSE PARTS
479 Whitehall Street SW
Atlanta, GA 30303
(404)577-5584
Plaster and cement cast columns and table bases

JO SONJA'S FOLK ART INC.
2136 Third Street
Eureka, CA 95501
(707)445-9306
Seminars, instruction books and supplies

LIBERTY PAINT CATALOGUE, INC.
P.O. Box 1248
Hudson, NY 12534
(518)828-4060
Faux finish brushes, tools, sponges and paints

LIBERTY STAIN AND VARNISH
26777 Lorain Road
North Olmstead, OH 44070
(216)779-5262
Stains and varnishes

LOEW-CORNELL, INC.
563 Chestnut Ave.
Teaneck, NJ 07666
(201)836-8110
Artists' and faux brushes

THE MAGIC BRUSH INC.
P.O. Box 868
Anthony, TX 79821
(505)233-4947
Seminars, instruction books and supplies

MARTIN/F. WEBER CO.
2727 Southampton Road
Philadelphia, PA 19154
(215)677-5600
Artists' paints, brushes and supplies

PARSONS COLLECTION, INC.
P.O. Box 52497
Atlanta, GA 30355
(404)261-1624
Wood furniture and accessories

PCM STUDIOS
731 Highland Ave. NE
Suite D
Atlanta, GA 30312
(404)222-0348
Seminars and instruction books

PRISCILLA'S
P.O. Box 521013
Tulsa, OK 74152
(918)743-6072
Seminars, instruction books and supplies

SCOTTIE'S BAVARIAN FOLK ART
6415 Rivington Road
Springfield, VA 22152
(703)569-2415
Seminars, instruction books and supplies

JACKIE SHAW STUDIO
Route 3
P.O. Box 155
Smithburg, MD 21783
(301)824-7592
Seminars and instruction books

ROBERT SIMMONS INC.
45 W. 18th Street
New York, NY 10011
(212)633-9237
Artists' brushes

SOCIETY OF DECORATIVE PAINTERS
P.O. Box 808
Newton, KS 67114
(316)283-9665
Membership organization, seminars and instruction books

STENCIL EASE
P.O. Box 1127
Old Saybrook, CT 06475
(203)395-0168
Stencils and supplies

UNFINISHED BUSINESS
P.O. Box 246
Wingate, NC 28174
(704)233-4295
Wood cut-outs and small accessories

WHIMSEY UNLIMITED
14672 Riverside Drive
Apple Valley, CA 92307
(619)996-1518
Seminars and instruction books

WINSOR & NEWTON
11 Constitution Ave.
Piscataway, NJ 08855
(201)562-0770
Artists' paints, brushes and supplies

CREDITS AND ACKNOWLEDGMENTS

The publisher and author would like to give credit and thanks to the individuals involved in creating this book.

All color and black-and-white step-by-step illustration artwork by Phillip C. Myer, photographed by Russell Brannon.

Painted finishes and decorative painting by Phillip C. Myer and photography by Russell Brannon, unless otherwise noted.

Page 98, the home of Mr. and Mrs. Tregellas, kitchen construction by Robert Trombetta Construction Services.

Page 99, decorative painting by Gretchen Cagle, the home of Phillip C. Myer.

Page 100 (top left), interior decoration by Murray Vise of J. Murray Vise Interior Design.

Page 100 (top right, bottom), interior decoration by Murray Vise of J. Murray Vise Interior Design; sponged walls by Barbara Lehman, The Painted Finish.

Page 101, interior decoration by Murray Vise of J. Murray Vise Interior Design.

Pages 102 and 103, the home of Mr. and Mrs. Kaiser, interior decoration by Jo Rabaut of Rabaut Design Associates.

Page 104 (both photos), painted finishes by Andy Jones, the home of Mr. and Mrs. Wood; interior decoration by Carter Arnest of R. Carter Arnest Ltd.

Page 105 (both photos), painted finishes by Andy Jones, Ann Jones, Joyce Beebe and Phillip C. Myer, in Mrs. Annella Schomburger's The Secret Garden Restaurant of Annella's; interior decoration by Ruth Bass of Bass and Bass Ltd.

Page 106 (both photos), painted finishes by Andy Jones, the home of Mr. and Mrs. Rimes.

Page 107 (both photos), painted finishes by Andy Jones, the home of Mr. and Mrs. Ouzts; interior decoration by Denise Ouzts.

Page 108 (both photos), painted finishes by Andy Jones, the home of Mr. and Mrs. Davis; interior decoration by Carter Arnest of R. Carter Arnest Ltd.

Page 109 (top), painted finishes by Terry Johnson, Michael LaRiche and Phillip C. Myer; photography by Michael LaRiche, the home of Michael LaRiche.

Page 109 (bottom), photography by Michael LaRiche, the home of Michael LaRiche.

Page 110, the home of Phillip C. Myer.

Page 111, painted finishes by Andy Jones and Phillip C. Myer.

Page 112, painted finishes by Chris Williams, the home of Mr. and Mrs. Renz.

Page 113 (both photos), the home of Mr. and Mrs. Nail.

Page 114, painted finishes by Chris Williams, the Strickland House of Mr. and Mrs. Zeigler.

Page 115, in the Newnan, GA 1990 Decorator Showhouse, photography by Bob Shapiro, interior decoration by The Jefferson House.

Page 116, decorative painting by Andy Jones and Phillip C. Myer.

Pages 117-126, decorative painting by Phillip C. Myer, photography by Russell Brannon.

Pages 127 and 128, Charles Keath Limited, photography by Don Matter.

Page 129, decorative painting and painted finishes by Phillip C. Myer, photography by Russell Brannon.

INDEX

Skippyjon Jones
CLASS ACTION

JUDY SCHACHNER

• DUTTON CHILDREN'S BOOKS •
AN IMPRINT OF PENGUIN GROUP (USA) INC.

To Nora Kate O'Sullivan, a true Spanish lass—
Love, Judy

My gratitude to all of Team Skippy,
and thanks to Cha Cha, the biggest of the small ones in the mirror,
and in memory of Mitzi Ambrose.

DUTTON CHILDREN'S BOOKS
A division of Penguin Young Readers Group

PUBLISHED BY THE PENGUIN GROUP
Penguin Group (USA) Inc., 375 Hudson Street, New York, New York 10014, U.S.A. • Penguin Group (Canada), 90 Eglinton Avenue East, Suite 700, Toronto, Ontario M4P 2Y3, Canada (a division of Pearson Penguin Canada Inc.) • Penguin Books Ltd, 80 Strand, London WC2R 0RL, England • Penguin Ireland, 25 St Stephen's Green, Dublin 2, Ireland (a division of Penguin Books Ltd) • Penguin Group (Australia), 250 Camberwell Road, Camberwell, Victoria 3124, Australia (a division of Pearson Australia Group Pty Ltd) • Penguin Books India Pvt Ltd, 11 Community Centre, Panchsheel Park, New Delhi - 110 017, India • Penguin Group (NZ), 67 Apollo Drive, Rosedale, Auckland 0632, New Zealand (a division of Pearson New Zealand Ltd) • Penguin Books (South Africa) (Pty) Ltd, 24 Sturdee Avenue, Rosebank, Johannesburg 2196, South Africa • Penguin Books Ltd, Registered Offices: 80 Strand, London WC2R 0RL, England

This special edition was printed for Kohl's Department Stores, Inc. (for distribution on behalf of Kohl's Cares, LLC, its wholly owned subsidiary) by Dutton Children's Books, a division of Penguin Young Readers Group.

Kohl's • 978-0-8037-3885-0 • 123386 • 02/12–07/12

Copyright © 2011 by Judith Byron Schachner • All rights reserved.

CIP Data is available.
This edition ISBN 978-0-8037-3885-0

Published in the United States by Dutton Children's Books, a division of Penguin Young Readers Group, 345 Hudson Street, New York, New York 10014
www.penguin.com/youngreaders

Designed by Heather Wood • Manufactured in China

1 2 3 4 5 6 7 8 9 10 • First Edition

The illustrations for this book were created in acrylics and pen and ink on Aquarelle Arches watercolor paper.

Skippyjon Jones was just dying to go to school.

And nobody, not even his mama, was going to stop him. But she did, by the scruff of his neck.

"School is for the DOGS!"
stated Mama Junebug Jones emphatically.

"They're *unruly*
and *drooly*,"
she added dramatically.

"Just *listen* to that barking—
those hounds sound

ferocious."

"Plus a bus full of dog breath would smell so **atrocious**.

Good golly, pop lollie! It's such a **no-brainer**.

If there is a good dog, it's because of its *trainer*."

His mama gently nudged her nugget into his room.

Then she added, "You're Skippyjon Jones, a smart Siamese cat. Take a look in the mirror if you don't believe that."

"He looks in the mirror every day," said his sisters, Jezebel, Jilly Boo, and Ju-Ju Bee, "but all he sees are Chi-wa-las."

"*Arff, arff,*" barked Ju-Ju Bee.

After his family left him to think, the Chi-wa-la did exactly what his mama suggested.

But not before he bounced around his room with some books.

"Oh, I'm *Skippyjonjones*,

And I don't get the fuss.

"It's not like a pigeon

Is driving the bus."

Then he climbed up his sisters' kitty-condo
ladder for a peekaboo in the mirror.

"Holy Julio!" squealed the kitty boy.

"How many Chihuahuas am I?" he wondered out loud.

Then he took a deep breath and, using his very best Spanish accent, he answered, "As many as your head can handle, *hombre*."

My Darling Boy
Think.
Siamese!
♡ mama

And quicker than you can say "the cat in the hat never did that," the kitty boy tossed his mask and his cape and a bright yellow banana into his *mochila*. Then, as he buttoned up his red plaid shirt, he began to sing in a *muy, muy* soft voice.

"Oh, my name is Skippito Friskito, (clap-clap)

And I'm off to the school for perritos, (clap-clap)

'Cuz I've got a good hunch

That I'm going to have lunch

With a grande ol' bunch of poochitos." (clap-clap)

Just across the hall, Mama Junebug Jones and the girls were doing a little homework of their own.

"Listen here, Messy Missies," said Mama, "how are you supposed to clean your kitty condo without your ladder?"

"Skippyjon has it," said the sisters.

"What for?" asked Mama.

"So he can see the Chi-wa-la in the mirror."

The Chi-wa-la, however, was already in his closet, boarding a bus for school.

But the kitty boy wasn't the only Chihuahua on board. His old *amigos*, Los Chimichangos, were going to school, too.

"Thank dog you made it, dude!" exclaimed Don Diego, the biggest of the small ones.

BARKER • ACADEMY

"*Sí*, Skippito," panted Poquito Tito, the smallest of the small ones. "We need your help *con el* bull-ito."

"Without a doubt-ito," declared El Skippito. "But why do you need my help with the bully?"

"Because he is a *perro mezquino*," declared Don Diego, "who *barrenas* around the *escuela* in a *tazalita*."

"He spins around the school in a **tiny teacup?**" exclaimed the kitty boy in shock.

"*Sí*, dude," added Don Diego. "He growls and howls and wears a *suérte de lana también*."

"Not the WOOL sweater," said Skippito.

"Uh-huh," agreed Poquito Tito, trembling. "He is a woolly bully."

There wasn't
a dog worth his biscuits
who didn't fear the woolly bully,
so it wasn't a surprise when a potent
puff of panic poofed out the *gatito*'s tail.

And all that puffiness inspired the
poochitos to sing:

"Oh, Puff-ee, Puff-oo, Puff-ito,
(clap-clap)
We know you can do it, Skippito.
(clap-clap)
Let's unravel his sweater
And knit something better.
We'll show that old woolly bull-ito."
(clap-clap)

But there was no turning back now.
The doggies had arrived at school.

A moment later, the principal,
a poodle with very high standards,
appeared with a bucket of balls
and a whistle.

First she BLEW.

And then she
THREW!

"Go fetch!"
barked Mrs. Begalot.

Then every dog, big and small, chased a ball
down the hall and into their classrooms.
Except for Skippito. He got carried along by
the river of rovers and . . .

. . . landed in art class where he drew his best ever double doggie doodle.

"I've never seen a pup do that before," said Mrs. Houndler, the art teacher.

Then he trotted over to the music room and bayed like a beagle for the canine chorus.

"Bow-*WOW!*" woofed Mr. Muzzletuff. "What a pair of ears."

0 1 2 3 4 5 6 7 8 9

After music came math, where Skippy stunned Mrs. McDrooler
with his counting skills.

"Two . . . three . . . five . . . seven . . . eleven."

ChubinA
 1
+1
 2

Poquito
Tito
3026
+2043
 5069

Ickky
 2
+2
 4

Snubs
 5
+5
 10

At the bell, the *amigos* followed their noses into the library.
Not even a bowl full of *frijoles* smelled as delicious as the scent of
books waiting to be read.

"I lick *libros*!" declared El Skippito Friskito, the great reader-ito.
"I like books, too," whispered Leonora Lappsitter, the librarian,
from behind the bookcase.

The kitty boy was the last to leave the library, so he had to race right over to French class with Monsieur Foozay.

"Can you say *cheese*?" asked the teacher.

"*Oui, oui!*" said zee poodles. "*Fromage.*"

"*Sí, sí,*" said Skippito. "*¡Queso!*"

"*¡Queso Cabeza!*" shouted the Chimichangos from the rear of the room.

"I'm not a cheese head, Chimichangos!" chuckled the
gatito. "I'm a Chihuahua!"

The poodles were tickled pink to have *los* poochitos
in class with them. And *los* poochitos wanted to share
what they had learned
with their *amigo*.

Zo zee poopies zang:

"Comme-çi, Comme-ça, Comme-cito (clap-clap)

we have zumzing to tell you, Skippito.

When zee poodles say Oui, (clap-clap)

zay really mean Sí,

*So don't look for a red
hydrant-ito!"* (clap-clap)

After French, *los muchachos* took a pass on Obedience Class, deciding instead to nap inside the warm case with the golden *trofeos*.

"I'm not good at following rules," confessed the kitty boy.

"What dog *IS*, dude?" quipped Don Diego.

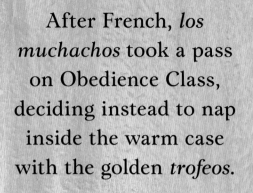

But just then, the *gatito* heard a gut-gurgling growl that shook the entire *escuela*, perhaps the whole *planeta*.

"Holy heartburn!" hollered Skippito. "Was that my tummy?"

"No. That is the bellow of the woolly bull-ito," said Poquito Tito with a shiver-ito.

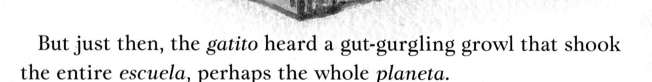

The gruesome grumble grew
louder, and along with it came the
rattle and plink of the terrible *tazalita*.
It was spinning wildly, right under his nose,
circling like a polka-dotted shark.

"*¡Andele!*" declared Don Diego. "Get out your duds, dude."
But Skippito was too frozen with fear to unpack his *mochila*. So his
amigos did it for him, helping to change their *chico* into El Skippito
Friskito, complete with mask, cape, and banana.

"Why the *plátano*, dude?" asked Pinto Lito.
"It's my snack-ito," replied the *gatito*.
"Will you share it with me and Tito?"
"Yes, indeed-o," agreed Skippito.

Then *woof* *chuck-a-luck-a-luck-a,* *woof* *chuck-a-luck-a-luck-a,* every doggie leaped out of the case and latched onto the turbo-charged *taza.*

This caused the cup to spin wildly out of control, some of the *chicos* just hanging on by a tail.

"*Estoy mareado,*" cried Skippito.

"You are not dizzy, dude, you're **green**," yipped the doggies.

The whirling dervish of a dog-filled teacup cut a mean path of destruction past the principal's office and spun straight on into the lunch bunch like a bowling ball.

"**Strike-ito!**" shouted the poochitos.

And strike it did.

Smash! Crackle! and Pop!

The twirling *tazalita* crashed right into a table and broke apart, exposing the fur-rocious fuzzy for what he really was—a teeny-tiny, itsy-bitsy, wool-wearing teacup Chihuahua.

"Dude!" declared Skippito. "You're no bigger than a bug-ito!"

But the bug-ito's only reply was a gut-gurgling growl greater than the hounds had ever heard before.

"Is that your tummy?" asked Skippito.

"*Sí*," replied the bull-ito. "*Tengo mucho hambre.*"

"I am hungry, too," agreed the *gatito*, "but you can have my *plátano.*"

This act of kindness made the Chimichangos pull
out their jump rope right in the middle of the mess.

Peanut butter and belly buttons,

Chunky cherry pits,

The woolly bully's taza

Has broken into bits!

Wiggle-waggle, wiggle-waggle,

Jelly on the toast,

He's not a woolly bully.

He's just hungrier than most!

Just then, Mrs. Begalot stomped into the lunchroom.
"I smell a cat!" she bellowed. "That cat better scat!"

Then out came the whistle.

First she BLEW,
          and then she THREW
a bright yellow ball down the hall, which
every dog, big and small, began to chase.
Except for Skippito. He wasn't chasing
the ball. He was running for his life.

First Skippy TRIPPED,
                then he SLIPPED
on the banana peel and slid straight out of
his closet . . .

. . . and back into the arms of
his Mama Junebug Jones.

"What in the woolly white
willies have you been up to,
Mr. Whistle Whiskers?"
asked Mama.

"He broke my teacup,"
whined Jilly Boo.

"And he ate my banana,"
complained Jezebel.

"That's 'cuz he went to
school with the Chi-wa-las,"
explained Ju-Ju Bee.

Later that night, after every fuzzy fell asleep,
the kitty boy was good for one last bounce.

"Oh, I'm Skippyjonjones,

And I couldn't say it better,

A dog is not a bully

Just because he wears a sweater!"

Then he bounced over to his mama and gave her a *beso*,
a kiss she felt straight through the layers of her quilt.
"Good night, Little Dipper," said the very sleepy mama.
"G'night, Mama," said the very sleepy kitten.